Theology Today
15 Why Were the Gospels Written?

Theology Today

GENERAL EDITOR:
EDWARD YARNOLD, S. J.

No. 15

Why Were the Gospels Written?

BY

JOHN ASHTON, S. J.

FIDES PUBLISHERS, INC.

NOTRE DAME, INDIANA

Nihil Obstat:

Jeremiah J. O'Sullivan, D.D.
Censor deputatus
11 November 1972

Imprimatur:

Cornelius Ep. Corag. & Ross
5 April 1973

ISBN 0 85342 261 3

ACKNOWLEDGEMENTS

The Scripture quotations in this publication are generally taken from the Revised Standard Version of the Bible, copyrighted 1946 and 1952 by the Division of Christian Education of the National Council of the Churches of Christ in the U.S.A. and used by kind permission. Thanks are also due to the following publishers: to the S.C.M. Press Ltd. for permission to quote from *The Phenomenon of the New Testament* by C.F.D. Moule, and from *New Testament Questions of Today* by E. Käsemann; to Penguin Books for permission to quote from *Saint Mark* by D.E. Nineham; to the Athlone Press for the use of the passages from *The New Testament and Rabbinic Judaism* by D. Daube; and to Faber and Faber for permission to reproduce the extract from *The Fourth Gospel* by E. Hoskyns.

CONTENTS

PREFACE

For many years Catholic biblical scholarship was strictly controlled by authority. This curtailment of freedom was not without its advantages: Catholics were saved from the confusion that was caused elsewhere by eccentric or ill-digested theories about the composition or the veracity of the scriptures. But the disadvantages were greater: not only was the faith of Catholics impoverished through being starved of the new insights into the meaning of God's word that responsible and unimpeded scholarship could afford; in addition obedience to authority degenerated into what almost amounted to a belief in the infallibility of the Biblical Commission.

Now all has changed: the activity of Catholic scripture scholars is in practice as free from constraint as that of other Christians. The result is that many Catholics have found themselves suddenly confronted with the unfamiliar suggestion that the truth of the Bible is not as straightforward as they had believed. This new uncertainty hits them hardest when the literal truth of the gospels seems to be in question. They feel that their faith is threatened, that they have been betrayed by the theologians.

Fr Ashton's book should help them to understand how the best of modern New Testament scholarship does not undermine Faith, but enriches it.

E. J. YARNOLD, S.J.

INTRODUCTION

In a series devoted to theology, there is no need to justify the inclusion of a book on the gospels. But perhaps the title of this one does call for a word of explanation. Why could it not have been called simply, 'The theology of the Gospels', to fall in line with the other titles of the series? There are two reasons: the first is that these set out to expound the Catholic tradition on some particular mystery of the faith. But the gospels are not just one topic among others: they are the well-spring of Christian teaching and preaching throughout the ages. Indeed, the Council of Trent did not hesitate to use the word 'gospel' to designate the ultimate source of the whole tradition. And although the great mysteries of the faith are all to be found, at least embryonically, in the gospels, there has never been a theology of the gospels in the sense in which there is a theology of the Trinity, of the Incarnation, or even of the act of faith. Hitherto, any *theology* of the gospels, any attempt, that is, to explain to Christian believers just what a gospel is, has been largely confined to the gospel writers themselves and a handful of modern exegetes. The gospels as such, unlike the Trinity and the Incarnation, have never constituted the material for systematic reflection.

The second reason for avoiding the title, *The theology of the Gospels* is that if it is taken (in the alternative sense) to mean not the theology *about* the gospels but the theology *contained in* the gospels, it is equally misleading. For the gospels are not works of theology, and the evangelists are not theologians, except in a very special sense which requires careful elucidation. The difference between St Paul and St John is not merely one of nuance and emphasis: St John was an evangelist, whereas St Paul was a letter-writing theologian. In the nineteenth century, people would have been surprised to hear the evangelists spoken of as theolo-

11

gians; today the expression has become commonplace. But though popular, it is inaccurate, or at any rate inadequate, as I hope to show in this book.

In so far as this little book is the product of a theological reflection upon the gospels, it might indeed have been called *A theology of the Gospels*, but it makes no claim whatever to set out the Church's teaching on the gospels (which is any way too sparse to provide material for a general work of this sort) in an authoritative way. There is, however, one document, published in 1964 by the Pontifical Biblical Commission, which provides such a convenient starting-point for our reflections that I propose to quote from it extensively here. The document is entitled *Instruction de historica Evangeliorum veritate* (Instruction concerning the historical truth of the gospels) but the title is misleading, since the word 'historical' does not occur in the body of the instruction.

In order to arrive at a sound assessment of the reliability of the gospel tradition, the exegete must take careful note of the three stages in which Jesus' life and teaching have come down to us.

(1) *Christ our Lord* gathered round him chosen disciples who followed him from the beginning, watching him act and hearing him speak, and were thus equipped to be witnesses of his life and teaching. In propounding his oral teaching, the Lord followed the methods of argument and exposition current in his day, accommodating himself to the mentality of his hearers and ensuring that what he taught would be firmly fixed and readily retained in the minds of his disciples. These men realised that the miracles and other events in Jesus' life were performed in the design of bringing men to believe in Christ and to embrace in faith the message of salvation.

(2) *The apostles'* main task was to proclaim the death and resurrection of the Lord, which they did by bearing witness to Jesus. They faithfully reported his life and utterances, taking into account in their meth-

od of preaching the circumstances in which their listeners were placed. After Jesus' resurrection, when his divinity was clearly perceived, the faith of these men, far from blotting out all memory of what had happened, actually strengthened their recollection, resting as it did upon Jesus' actual deeds and teaching. There is no question of his having been transformed into a 'mythical' personage, nor of his teaching having been distorted as a consequence of the worship paid to him from that time on by the disciples as Lord and Son of God. But there is no reason to deny that the apostles passed on to their hearers the actual words and deeds of the Lord with that fuller understanding which they enjoyed through having been instructed by the glorious events of the Christ and having been taught by the light of the Spirit of truth. So it is that just as Jesus himself 'interpreted to them' after the resurrection the words of the Old Testament as well as his own, they in their turn explained his words and deeds in a way suited to the requirements of their hearers. 'Devoting themselves to the ministry of the word' (Acts 6.4), they made use in their preaching of various methods of exposition suited both to their own purpose and to the mentality of their hearers; for they were indebted both 'to Greeks and non-Greeks, to the wise and to the foolish'. But the methods of exposition which those heralds of Christ used to proclaim him must be distinguished and properly assessed: catecheses, narratives, testimonia, hymns, doxologies, prayers, and other such literary forms, used both in sacred scripture and in other contemporary works.

(3) Finally, for the benefit of the churches, *the sacred writers* put this primitive teaching, which was at first passed on by word of mouth and later in writing, in the form of four gospels, each employing a method particularly suited to his aims; for it was not long before many attempts were made 'to compile a narrative of the things' concerning the Lord Jesus. Some of

13

the traditional material was selected, other parts compressed to a resumé, other parts still expanded, with an eye on the situation of the churches. And they took every possible step to ensure that their readers should acknowledge the reliability of the truths in which they were instructed. From the traditions they inherited the sacred writers picked out those which were suited to their own purposes and the various situations in which the faithful found themselves. And since the meaning of a statement also depends on what comes before and after, the evangelists placed the words and deeds of our Saviour in various different settings, always with a view to their readers' profit. This is why the exegete has to endeavour to discover what the evangelist intended by narrating a saying or event in a particular way or setting it in a particular context. The fact that the evangelists relate the words and deeds of the Lord in a different order, and whilst preserving their meaning give different (and not literally accurate) versions of his utterances, does nothing to impair the essential truth of the narrative. For as St Augustine remarked, 'It is quite likely that each of the evangelists believed himself bound to recount things in the order in which it pleased God to suggest them to his memory' – in those matters at any rate in which the order, whatever it was, could not detract from the truth and authority of the gospel. But with reasonable care and devotion anyone may enquire and, with the aid of God, discover why it is that the Holy Spirit, who bestows his gifts on whom he chooses, and who undoubtedly governed and controlled the minds of the holy writers in recalling what they were to write (because of the pre-eminent authority the books were to enjoy), permitted one to compile his narrative in this way, and another in that.

Unless the exegete pays attention to these factors, all of which affect the origin and composition of the gospels, and makes good use of all the laudable achievements of recent research, he will not be carrying out his task of probing into what the sacred writers meant and what they really said. From the results of recent investigations it is evident that the life and teaching of Jesus were not simply reported, so as not to be forgotten, but 'preached', so as to furnish the Church with a secure basis for her teaching, both doctrinal and moral. And so the exegete, by tirelessly scrutinizing the patrimony of the evangelists, will be in a position to show in greater depth the perennial theological value of the gospels and to exhibit clearly the importance and necessity of the interpretation the Church has put upon them [*Acta Apostolicae Sedis* 56 (1964) 712ff.].

Connoisseurs of Roman documents will recognize behind the clumsy and guarded language of this one a sincere acknowledgement of the advances made in the study of the gospels during the twentieth century and an encouragement to Catholic scholars to adopt methods of research whose implications are far-reaching indeed and which fifty years earlier would undoubtedly have been rejected out of hand. For corresponding to the three stages of revelation distinguished in this *Instruction* are three approaches to the study of the gospels. The first we may call 'the quest of the historical Jesus'. This approach dominated nineteenth-century scholarship. The second, which held undisputed sway, in Germany at any rate, between the two world-wars, is 'Form Criticism'. The third, currently the most popular, is 'Redaction Criticism'. Each of these approaches enjoys certain advantages and suffers from certain drawbacks. To focus one's attention too exclusively on one or other of the three stages of the tradition will inevitably result in one's having a lopsided view of the origins of the Christian tradition, and before commenting on the three stages in detail, I propose to say something about each of these highly influential approaches to the study of the gospels.

In the first two chapters, then, I shall attempt to comment upon the recent history of the exegesis of the gospels. Towards the end of the eighteenth century, the truth of the gospels was seriously questioned for the first time by men

15

who nevertheless continued to profess some sort of belief in Christianity. So during the following century exegetes and theologians were busy trying to find answers to the difficulties that had been raised. In Chapter 1, I shall try and give some account of the philosophical genesis of these difficulties as well as of some of the proposed solutions. Because of the nature of the material, this chapter may prove rather hard going to those without any knowledge of philosophy. The remainder of the book is, I trust, much simpler.

The beginning of this century saw a marked shift of attitude. Interest came to be focused less upon the source of the gospel tradition – Jesus' own life and teaching – than upon the development of that tradition within the Christian community, and subsequently upon the special preoccupations of the individual evangelists. These new approaches, known respectively as 'form criticism' and 'redaction criticism', are discussed in Chapter 2.

So much, then, for the general lines of modern scholarship. In the following chapter, I turn to a consideration of the gospel tradition itself, beginning with the first two stages, as outlined in the instruction of the Pontifical Biblical Commission I have just quoted. I regard this third chapter as very important.

Finally, after a chapter on the third stage of the tradition (The Evangelists, Chapter 4), I single out some salient aspects in each of the synoptic gospels (Chapter 5) and conclude with a chapter on the Fourth Gospel, which crowns the whole tradition.

THE QUEST OF THE HISTORICAL JESUS

The explicit distinction between the historical Jesus and the Christ of faith can shock the traditionally-minded, because it appears to suggests that these are two separate figures with no real continuity between them (and this is, in fact, more or less the view of Rudolf Bultmann, one of the founder-fathers of form criticism). The roots of this opposition reach right down into the eighteenth-century Enlightenment. Lessing, who six years earlier had begun to let loose upon a startled world the famous 'fragments of Reimarus (including that on 'The Aims of Jesus and his Disciples'), wrote in 1780 that 'contingent truths of history can never serve as the demonstration of eternal truths of reason.' It would scarcely be an exaggeration to say that the problems implicit in this dictum have dominated christological thinking (at least in so far as New Testament scholars indulge in such a pastime) ever since. And they are certainly with us still.

The nineteenth century quest originated, then, with Lessing's publication of Reimarus' sardonic and trenchant reflections on the gospels. And Albert Schweitzer's classic account of the quest, to which the English translator gave the colourful and evocative title, *The Quest of the Historical Jesus*, was called simply, in the original German edition of 1906, *Vom Reimarus zu Wrede* (from Reimarus to Wrede) – we shall meet Wrede again later on. Quite recently, Reinhardt Slenczka has shown (*Geschichtlichkeit und Personensein Jesu Christi*, 1967) that the motives Schweitzer attributes to the scholars of the nineteenthcentury are to a large extent fabricated out of his own prejudices, and that he consequently fails to do justice to the complexity of their preoccupations and concerns. So perhaps it would be wise to refrain here from imputing motives and to confine ourselves to outlining some of the effects of the nineteenthcentury

17

search for an accurate and lifelike portrait of the historical Jesus.

The dichotomy disclosed by Lessing is one form of *the* crucial issue in philosophy, which is the relation between thought and being. Does thought constitute the real, or should it be determined by it? History is concerned in the first place with contingent truths. But how can these have a universal significance? Do we impose a pattern upon the facts which emerge from the historian's researches, or is the pattern already there? And if it is already there, how is it there? This issue did not begin to trouble Christian thinkers until they were confronted, in the nineteenth century, with the necessity of finding a *theological* solution to this fundamental problem. A number of writers, from David Friedrich Strauss (whose massive *Life of Jesus* was translated into English by no less a person than George Eliot) to Rudolf Bultmann, have chosen to play down the historical element in Christianity in favour of some position (myth or kerygma, it does not matter) which is thought to be in principle invulnerable to the unwelcome intrusions of historical research. In other words, they place themselves squarely on the 'thought' side of the thought-being relationship. Others, and until the advent of dialectical theology in Germany shortly after the 1914-18 war these were in the majority, preferred to base their faith on what they conceived to be the solid and reliable results of scholarly exegesis of the gospels.

It is the chief thesis of this little book that the dichotomy between the Jesus of history and the Christ of faith has somehow to be overcome if we are to arrive at a balanced interpretation of the gospels, considered here as early expressions of Christian belief. Just as the opposition between thought and being, if allowed to go unchallenged, can only lead to insoluble paradoxes like the Kantian antinomies, so the nineteenth-century scholars, who inherited the challenge of Reimarus and, later, of Strauss, suffered from a built-in handicap of which they were only partially aware. The camel had got his nose under the tent, and it was just a question of time before it toppled over completely. Catholic philosophers like Maréchal and Lonergan have attempted to solve the Kantian paradox with a new theory of the act of judgment; and it may well be that some such theory is required to anchor any theological refutation of Strauss and Bultmann. Fortunately, that cannot be our concern here.

The model of inspiration on which previous theologians had worked was blessedly free from such troublesome, sophisticated and, in the last analysis, artificial problems. For early Christian exegetes and theologians, the historical infrastructure and the spiritual interpretation they erected upon it were distinguishable, certainly, but not properly separable; and the sort of distinction they allowed, although analogous to the thought-being dichotomy of the Enlightenment, did not worry them unduly. Consider the earliest pictures that we have of the composition of the gospels, in Byzantine mosaics and the murals and manuscripts of the Middle Ages. We see Matthew, Mark, Luke or John seated pen in hand behind an awkward-looking table which appears as though it is about to let everything on it slide off onto the floor, and in the background a peculiar figure with the face of a lion, an ox, a man or an eagle as the case may be, though in most cases the artist has shrunk from portraying these exactly as they appear in the Book of Revelation, 'covered with eyes, in front and behind' (Apoc 4.6). Very often we see rays of light proceeding from some heavenly source, and we are clearly meant to understand that they are busy composing their several gospels under the direct inspiration of the Holy Spirit. No doubt they were believed to have described events accurately and faithfully, but the presence of emblems of the Spirit shows that in order to see the *spiritual* significance of what they were narrating they needed more than a good memory or a good eye for detail.

Nevertheless, the spiritual significance is not thought of as detached or detachable from the narrative. There is therefore a double kind of continuity – of report and of content: of report, because the evangelists were thought to have been either eye-witnesses of the events they were describing – Matthew and John – or else faithful, even slavish amanuenses – Mark and Luke, the companions of Paul, one of whom is said to have also been a close follower of Peter, and the other, at least according to one tradition, of Mary, the Mother of the Lord. And also, even more importantly, of content: the spiritual significance of, for instance, the healing of the blind is inseparable from the physical events on which it rests; where Jesus is credited with an especially perspicacious saying, which illuminates the life of the primitive Christian community, this is in the first place because he foresaw precisely what their situation would be and in the second place because he always had a faithful scribe at his elbow who could be relied upon to transcribe his words accurately, or at any rate to recall them much later under the prompting of the Holy Spirit.

It might be objected that this description of the process of inspiration is sardonic and unfair, but the fact is that for centuries Christian readers were so close to the gospels, so directly aware of their power, truth and beauty, that they did not think of questioning the naive and symbolic view of their composition which they had before their eyes in pictures or manuscript illuminations. The two kinds of truth, historical and symbolic (or spiritual) were so tightly enmeshed that they did not *need* to try to disentangle them. But as early as the end of the seventeenth century (with the publication in 1678 of Richard Simon's *Histoire critique du Vieux Testament*) this uncritical acceptance of the theory of direct inspiration began to come under fire; and first the Old Testament and then the New were scrutinized by scholars, some sceptical, others believing, who arrived at a variety of conclusions concerning the mode of composition of the Bible and in particular concerning the interrelationships of the first three gospels.

The gloriously imaginative allegorizing of the early Fathers (Origen and the school of Alexandria in particular) did, it is true, come in for a good deal of criticism. The poet Donne, for instance, clearly enjoyed satirizing it in his sermons and other prose writings. But it was not the Renaissance (which had gone in for a fair amount of allegorizing of its own, in painting as well as in poetry) but the eighteenth-century Enlightenment that drove the most effective wedge between the literal or historical and the spiritual significance of the Bible, and the results of this separation, as we have observed, lasted throughout the nineteenth century.

They were especially keenly felt in the field of gospel criticism, and towards the end of the century they were exposed and discarded by Martin Kähler in his celebrated lecture, *The so-called Historical Jesus and the Historic, Biblical Christ* (Fortress Press, Philadelphia, 1960), the length of which causes one to reflect admiringly on the sheer staying-power of nineteenth-century audiences. The lecture hinges upon the opposition between two German words, *'historisch'* and *'geschichtlich'*. In view of the fact that Kähler himself quite frequently uses *'geschichtlich'* in the sense he assigns to *'historisch'*, this opposition must be said to be somewhat arbitrary, but for all that it is extremely important. The first word, *'historisch'* is applied to anything in principle discoverable by historical research: if you hold, with von Ranke, that the purpose of history is to find out 'what actually happened', and that it is possible, at least in principle, so to sift and assess the historical sources one is using as to obtain a completely impartial view of events that took place long ago and of the people who participated in them, then you might wish to say that what holds for Caesar and Napoleon must also hold for Jesus, and that it ought to be possible, in reading the gospels, to discount the natural bias of the evangelists, writing in the light of the resurrection, and to construct a reasonably accurate picture of the man Jesus and of the main events of his life.

The second word, *'geschichtlich'*, is more complex. Kähler uses it almost in the sense of 'real', and indeed in some versions of the title it is rendered by two words, 'real, historic' as opposed to 'historical'. The real Christ is he who is proclaimed by the apostles, the Christ of faith, who is also the 'biblical' Christ, in whom the Scriptures have found their fulfilment. He is *historic* in the sense of Croce's famous aphorism, taken over by Collingwood, 'all history is contemporary history', and not as a historical personage detachable from the impact that he makes in the present, upon Christian believers here and now. 'The reason we commune with the Je-

21

sus of our Gospels,' says Kähler, 'is because it is through them that we learn to know that same Jesus whom, with the eyes of faith and in our prayers, we meet at the right hand of God, because we know, with Luther, that God cannot be found except in his beloved Son, because he is God's revelation to us, or, more accurately and specifically, because he who once walked on earth and now is exalted is the incarnate Word of God, the image of the invisible God – because he is for us God revealed' (*op. cit.* p. 60f.).

Subsequently, the word '*geschichtlich*' was either enriched with connotations of existential challenge or else dropped altogether in favour of the word 'kerygmatic', which does much the same job. 'What is a truly 'historic figure', that is, a person who has been influential in molding posterity, as measured by his contribution to history? Is it not the person who originates and bequeaths a permanent influence?... The person whom history remembers lives on through his work' (p. 63). And in this sense the historic Christ is the Risen Christ, 'who has exercised an influence in history, with whom millions have communed in childlike faith, and with whom the great witnesses of the faith have been in communion – while striving, apprehending, triumphing and proclaiming – *this real Christ is the Christ who is preached*' (p. 66). And it is evident that the power and authority of the Risen Lord whom Christians worship is infinitely greater than that of the historical Jesus who walked the hills of Galilee and the streets of Jerusalem.

Kähler's view, then, was that the real living Christ is the Christ of faith, and that consequently the whole gigantic effort to discover the original traits of the historical Jesus was dangerous and misguided. But he also argued that the historical Jesus was so overlaid with dogmatic interpretations about him that the search was doomed to failure from the outset, if, at any rate, its object was to remove the upper layers of interpretation so as to disclose a portrait uncontaminated by later accretions.

There are therefore two separate questions that may be put concerning the quest for the historical Jesus: first of all is it *necessary* or *desirable*; and secondly is it *possible* to strip away the accumulations of time and lay bare the authentic life and teaching of Jesus of Nazareth? And it is obvious that the two questions can receive different answers: if it were felt to be desirable to pursue the quest, it would not follow that it must be possible to carry it through to a successful conclusion; conversely, the sheer possibility of discovering the authentic lineaments of the historical Jesus would not necessarily imply that the portrait of Jesus thus disclosed would be a necessary or even a desirable element in the Christian faith. Authors such as J.M. Robinson, in his valuable book, *The New Quest of the Historical Jesus* (1959), are quite right, then, to distinguish between the possibility and the legitimacy of the original quest.

Let us see how Kähler viewed these questions. His first insight concerned the legitimacy of the original quest. 'The historical Jesus of modern writers,' he announced, 'blocks the living Christ from our view.' Kähler was struck by the enormity of the historians' pretensions. It seemed to him that behind their earnest apologetic intentions lay a claim too staggering ever to receive precise formulation; namely that the Christian faith really depended upon their labours. 'How can Jesus Christ be the authentic object of the faith of all Christians,' he asks, 'if the questions who and what he really was can be established only by ingenious investigation and if it is solely the scholarship of our time which proves itself equal to this task?' (p. 102). Even supposing that it were possible for the historians to dispel the mists which have come to obscure the lineaments of the historical Jesus, what must be said of our forefathers in the faith, who enjoyed no such privilege? 'They would not have known their Savior' (p. 61). Kähler resists this conclusion with all his might. No one can tell us where to look for a 'fifth evangelist capable of providing us with the picture of the exalted Christ, the picture of God revealed' (p. 62). Reflecting on the extraordinary shifts of critical opinion, he remarks that 'the outlines and actual features of his life vary continuously with the changing results of biblical research. If questions like that of Jesus' sinlessness, of the clarity of his self-estimate or of his messianic consciousness, of "the idea of the Second Coming", of his lordship over history, or of his seat at the right hand of the Father, must first pass through the filigree of historical evaluation and application of the Gospel materials, then the question arises: How can this figure of Jesus, this tentative residue remaining after the work of critical subtraction, which must now, for the first time, be ingeniously evoked from the mist of the past, be the object of faith for all Christians?' (p. 103). Certainly faith does not depend upon a christological dogma. But it is just as erroneous to make it depend on uncertain statements about an allegedly reliable picture of Jesus that has been tortuously extracted by the modern methods of historical research' (p. 72f.).

But as well as illegitimate, the quest was fruitless. It was impossible to separate out the historical Jesus from the Christ of faith because all our sources are composed from the vantage point of Easter, and interpret all Jesus' words and works in the light of the resurrection: 'The risen Lord is not the historical Jesus *behind* the Gospels, but the Christ of the apostolic preaching, of the *whole* New Testament' (p. 65). The gospels, which are virtually the only possible source of information for facts about Jesus, are not history books or biographies but something closer to sermons. Kähler's contemporaries might have admitted this as far as Matthew and Luke were concerned, but at the time he wrote it still seemed a plausible hypothesis that some sort of biographical tradition could be extracted from Mark.

And in fact Kähler did leave some room for a recognizable human portrait of Jesus:

Nevertheless, from these fragmentary traditions, these half-understood recollections, these portrayals colored by the writers' individual personalities, these heartfelt confessions, these sermons proclaiming him as Savior, there gazes upon us a vivid and coherent image of a Man, an image we never fail to recognize. Hence, we may conclude that in his unique and powerful personality and by his incomparable deeds and life (including his resurrection appearances) this Man has engraved his image on the mind and memory of his followers with such sharp and deeply etched features that it could be neither obliterated nor distorted. If we are drawn up short by this mystery, then we must recall that he himself solved it in advance when he said: 'When the Spirit of truth comes... he will glorify me, for he will take what is mine and declare it to you (Jn 16.13f.). (Kähler, *op. cit.* p. 89f.)

In this quotation from John, Kähler has stumbled upon what I believe to be the true solution to the whole problem. I say, 'stumbled upon', for, as far as I can see, Kähler never really succeeded in shaking himself free from the nineteenth-century problematic. In opting for 'the historic Christ' rather than 'the historical Jesus', he was simply hanging his theological hat on the other horn of the dilemma. Though he was aware of the crucial question posed by Lessing's formula, he never quite managed to resolve it. Nevertheless, his lecture remains a powerful and convincing critique of the nineteenth-century quest.

I shall be arguing later that there is a certain biographical interest in the gospels, and that it is integral to their purpose. It would be foolish to minimize the force of Kähler's arguments against those scholars who saw themselves as picture-restorers, endeavouring to scrape the dirt of ages from the portrait of Jesus. But to restrict one's interest in the gospels to the information they can be made to yield about Jesus' actual words and deeds is to neglect their real message. It is like reading Shakespeare's 'historical' plays as historical source-books. No doubt much can be learnt from *Richard II* about Richard II (and if there were no other sources available, historians would be forced to make more use of it than they do). But that is not the point or purpose of the play. In assessing the merits of *Richard II*, historical accuracy is in itself irrelevant, although it is evident that the traditions on which Shakespeare based his play, and which can be said to have furnished the original 'inspiration' of his own character-study, orginated in the physical existence of the king himself. To that extent, the connection between the historical Richard and the stage Richard can be said to be a necessary one.

Not that this comparison can be pressed is every detail. The original inspiration of the gospels is not definable in terms of human genius: it was the experience of the resurrection. But it is just as true of the evangelists as it is of Shakespeare that their primary intention was not to convey information or to furnish material for subsequent historians. Besides, the purely biographical approach to the study of the gospels had very unfortunate consequences on the level of popular spirituality. A cursory examination of religious attitudes in the nineteenth century shows them to be pervaded by a kind of sentimental *mimesis:* Christ was regarded above all as a model of human behaviour and the basic relationship of the believer towards him was one of unreflecting imitation. The evangelical pietism of Lutheran Germany (above all of the sect known as the Moravians), the meditation-manuals up till recently inflicted on young religious by well-meaning superiors, the dreary and voluminous writings of the convert Faber, the wishy-washy paintings of pre-Raphaelites like Holman Hunt – all are infected by the same blight. The attitude I have qualified as 'mimesis' represents a radical impoverishment of the Christian tradition, and it proved fair game both for the Catholic modernists at the turn of the century and for Protestant dialectical theology a little later. To try and isolate the historical substratum beneath the proclamation of the evangelists is like trying to squeeze the cream out of butter: the gospels are written, according to a phrase of St Paul taken over by Johannes Weiss and used repeatedly in this connection ever since, 'from faith to faith'. Their purpose is to evoke and sustain belief, not just to paint the portrait of man for us to admire and imitate.

CHAPTER 2

FORM CRITICISM AND REDACTION CRITICISM

Form Criticism

When the form critics appeared at the end of the 1914-1918 war to hold out a new technique and a new approach to the gospels, they received a warm welcome. Traditional exegesis, as we have seen, had held the events and conversations recorded in the gospels and their spiritual interpretation in a close and unfussy unity. The nineteenth-century quest had concentrated chiefly upon rediscovering the factual substratum of the gospels. The form critics, relying partly on the earlier work of Wellhausen and Wrede, argued that the efforts of the nineteenth-century historians were largely a waste of time, and that it is impossible to know more than a few insignificant details about the actual life and personality of Jesus of Nazareth. They maintained that the gospels were not really the work of Jesus' personal disciples, in spite of the tradition to that effect, but of the early Church, which adapted traditions and what Bultmann calls 'legends' for their own purposes, chiefly liturgical and catechetical.

It is important to grasp that form criticism is first of all a *method*, only secondarily a doctrine. The method was adopted from an Old Testament scholar called Hermann Gunkel, who had argued twenty years earlier that within the Old Testament – and even within a single book, Genesis, say, or the Book of Psalms – several different *kinds* of writing can be discerned. Many psalms, for instance, are psalms of praise, others psalms of supplication; then there are entrance psalms, wisdom psalms, royal psalms, and so on.

A more modern example will help to make the point clearer. Suppose that I happen to be walking along the street when a particularly nasty accident occurs, which shocks me profoundly. I am summoned to appear in court as a witness

27

in an action brought against one of the people involved; I send a telegram to a friend to explain why I can't visit him as I had promised; I write a letter to another friend describing the incident. The court report, the telegram and the letter are all concerned with the same event; but the way in which the successive features of the incident are deployed will be different in each case. The telegram will be very brief; the report of the trial will be in question-and-answer form; the letter will recount both the accident and my reactions to it. If I am a poet I may jot something down in my diary for future incorporation in a poem; if I am a preacher I may use the incident as an object-lesson to help me emphasize the duty of behaving responsibly and with due thought for others, or the unpredictability of life or the mysterious ways of providence. The diary jotting, the poem, and the sermon will once again be different from the telegram, the letter and the transcript of the trial. Now the word 'form' in form criticism refers to nothing more complicated than this: we can, if we like, think of innumerable *literary* forms (the play, the novel, the short story, the essay), but these are all art-forms, whereas the form in form criticism is what Bultmann calls a sociological concept; it arises spontaneously out of the situation in which I find myself: I utilize it because it happens to lie ready to hand. The letter, the diary and the telegram are all generally accepted ways of expression; the court-trial is a feature of the life of civilized society; even the sermon is a traditional form of communication.

So the form, in the sense in which the form critics took the word, is very closely integrated within the life of the society in which it is exercised; and to understand its exercise it is far more important to know the *general* concerns of the society and its habitual patterns of behaviour than to know the subject-matter, the content, which, as we have seen, can be expressed in any number of different ways. The situation to which a particular literary form corresponds, and in which, as it were, the factual or other content of what is recorded seeks expression, is called in German *Sitz-im-Leben*, an untranslatable expression that has received a number of different renderings in English, of which 'setting in life' is perhaps the least misleading and tendentious. In the case of a sermon, the *Sitz-im-Leben* is a religious service, in the case of the trial evidence a courtroom and the whole tradition of the English judiciary. The letter, the diary jotting and the telegram, were they to be studied by a historian belonging to a totally alien culture, would have to be explained by reference to the *Sitz-im-Leben* of each, just as, let us say, the Homeric poems were not properly understood until it was discovered that they belonged to the genre of bardic poetry, that they were composed to be recited orally and were transmitted by generations of wandering poets until one version was finally set down on paper.

This point is worth emphasizing because it is often inadequately grasped or missed altogether. 'Literary form' and '*Sitz-im-Leben*' are correlative terms. One cannot study the one without studying the other, though it is possible to start from either. In the preface to the second edition of his standard work on form criticism, Bultmann describes the difference between his own approach and that of Dibelius:

> It is essential to realize that form criticism is fundamentally indistinguishable from all historical work in this, that it has to move in the influences operating in the life of the community, and the life of the community must be used to render the forms themselves intelligible. There is no method of regulating or even prescribing the necessary interplay and mutual relationships of both these processes, no rule to say where the start must be made. When M. Dibelius pursues his 'Constructive Method', i.e. when he reconstructs the history of the synoptic tradition from a study of the community and its needs; and when, contrariwise, I proceed from the analysis of the particular elements of the tradition, we are not opposed the each other, but rather engaged in mutually complementary and corrective work. Dibelius can no more get a clear idea of the motives of the life of the community without first making some inquiry about forms, than I, in my analysis, can dispense with a provisional picture of

the primitive community and its history, which has to be turned into a clear and articulated picture in the course of my inquiries (*The History of the Synoptic Tradition*[2], p. 5).

So one cannot understand a literary form like the oral epic without understanding the purpose and circumstances of its recitation. And *Sitz-im-Leben* is not just a fancy way of referring to the historical circumstances in which a particular sermon was preached or a particular letter written: it is the cultural background of the genre 'sermon' or the genre 'letter' as the case may be.

And this is a further point that needs to be fully appreciated if the real range and focus of form criticism is to be properly understood. What one may, with due reservations, call the historical nucleus of what ultimately finds expression in one or other literary form is inaccessible to the form-critical method as such and left unilluminated by its beam. To apply form-critical methods to the study of a letter or telegram telling of a street accident would not help to determine when and where the accident took place. Form criticism alone will not tell me when the Homeric poems were composed, still less when the events they describe occurred. Too often the form critics move from the true observation that such and such a form must be the work of the primitive community, for it corresponds to situations that Jesus simply would not have come up against, to the false conclusion that the core of the saying or narrative must also be ascribed to the creative fertility of the early Church. This may be so, but it must be argued in each case, and argued along lines that must entail the application of other than purely form-critical methods.

However, the contention of the form critics is that the *Sitz-im-Leben* of the vast majority of the literary forms distinguishable in the gospels and Acts is to be sought, not in the situation of an itinerant preacher in first-century Palestine, but in the life of the Christian community, practising its own faith and endeavouring to convey its faith to others. Consequently we are forced to draw a distinction between the form-critical *method* and the sphere in which it is exercised. The method as such is not confined to the Bible: it could equally well be extended to the study of Roman law or medieval mystery plays. But since it was elaborated largely by exegetes, especially Gunkel, who was something of a genius, it has come to be associated primarily, if not exclusively, with the study of the Old and New Testaments. But the postulate that it is to the Christian community and not to the life of Jesus that we must turn to discover the *Sitz-im-Leben* of the various literary forms within the pages of the gospels, needs to be proved and tested in each individual case. In fact, it very quickly came to be treated almost as an axiom by the form-critical school, and so it becomes necessary to distinguish between form-criticism as a method (which has no more axioms than a microscope) and as a doctrine. The method, as I have insisted, always comprises a study of two interrelated elements, literary form and *Sitz-im-Leben*. As a method, it has much to be said for it, although it is not an all-purpose tool: there are some jobs it cannot tackle. As a doctrine, it is very questionable indeed, although it is probably nearer the truth than the doctrine it set out to challenge, viz. that in the gospels we have authentic and eye-witness reports of the actual words and works of Jesus.

I shall have to confine my illustration of form criticism to a single example, drawn from what Bultmann calls 'the Tradition of the Saying of Jesus' (as opposed to 'the Tradition of the Narrative Material'), and illustrating how much light can be shed on the gospels by a study that takes into account the probable situation of the community in which the traditions were given expression. Among the type of sayings known in English (after Vincent Taylor's *The Formation of the Gospel Tradition*, 1973) as 'pronouncement stories', which consist of a retort or maxim embedded in a tiny narrative, there are a number of 'controversy dialogues' (a form abundantly illustrated in near-contemporary rabbinical texts). Several examples of these are to be found in Mk 2.1. 3.6. They can be analysed, from a literary point of view, into three parts: (1) Jesus or his disciples perform a revolutionary action ('One sabbath he was going through

31

the grainfields; and as they made their way his disciples began to pluck ears of grain'); (2) the Pharisees remonstrate with him – or, on occasion, merely 'marvel' ('And the Pharisees said to him, "Look, why are they doing what is not lawful on the sabbath?" '); and (3) he silences them with a devastating retort ('Have you never read what David did, when he was in need and was hungry...?').

Now the legal historian David Daube remarks that stories told in this way are to be found in all literature: 'Any newspaper may report: "Mrs X refused to fill in the census-paper, an official went to see her, but she told him that as she had kept her age a secret from her husband she was not going to divulge it to Mr Attlee." ' And he adds that the structure reflected by this situation constantly recurs in everyday life: 'It is indeed a special case of what must be one of the oldest, simplest and most frequent types of conversation: unusual conduct – question – explanation'. But he goes on to point out that it is not enough, in the case of the synoptics, where the form is recurrent, to say that it is a natural form. 'It is precisely this fact,' he says, 'which needs to be investigated: what do we mean by declaring it natural, what is the setting in life of which it appears the only fitting expression, in what situation would it be so popular as to be used again and again?' In answering this question, he remarks that 'the direct, dramatic presentation of revolutionary action, protest and silencing of the remonstrants – as opposed, say, to a more detached, academic record of events – is no doubt meant for a public still in a state of active, lively controversy with the Pharisees, and strongly feeling the need of refuting the troublesome enemy.' We cannot, I think, be sure from this fact alone that all these stories are rooted in the life of Jesus himself; but from a further observation of Daube's –namely that 'the third member (i.e. of the structure) describes the defeat of the Pharisees on their own ground, by an argument resting on a basis they themselves acknowledge,' – we can conclude with certainty that the form dates at the very latest 'from a time when it was vital to defend the ways of the new community – revolutionary actions – in a technical, scholarly, Pharisaical manner' *(The New Testament and Rabbinic Judaism,* (1956) pp. 170ff.).

The interest of this example is twofold. In the first place, it shows that the form-critical approach can render the reader more attentive to the details of the gospel narrative, make him more discriminating and sensitive to the shades of meaning and emphasis he encounters there and to the message of the text itself. In the second place, it shows in what way the *Sitz-im-Leben* can be isolated. The circumstances in which these stories received their formulation can be determined with considerable precision, and because of the contents of these particular stories, the place and period can to some extent be delimited also. Though the situation evoked is a natural one, the form, in spite of its simplicity, is largely artificial: it is a way of describing a fairly common occurrence with pungency and humour. But form criticism alone is unable to tell us whether the event described really took place at the time and place that are indicated, or even whether it took place at all and is not simply an edifying story. Most of the practitioners of form-criticism – and Daube is no exception – tend to assume that the story itself was an invention of the Christian community, but this, of course, is far from self-evident; and in the case of the parables it is often virtually certain that the original setting was Jesus' own career as a wandering prophet in Palestine.

In conclusion, it is important to realise that the general effect of form criticism was to reduce interest in the purpose of the final redactor and also in the events and sayings that presumably formed the stuff from which the various traditions were derived. It drove a wedge between Jesus and the evangelist, these two who for centuries had been thought to be so close, but instead of seeking to bridge the gap it thus disclosed, it devoted itself to the study of the gap itself. Consequently the period that received most critical attention between the wars, in Germany at any rate, was the period of what Vincent Taylor calls 'the Formation of the Gospel Tradition', which covered the years, say, 35-60 A.D. The reasons were partly practical and partly ideological. From a practical point of view, the method was seen to best advantage within a liberal tradition that was not held to defending the verbal accuracy of the gospel report. Among the ideological reasons may be numbered a reluctance, at least on Bultmann's part, to ground faith upon history (Bultmann speaks somewhere of the contentment with which he watched the fanciful portraits of the Life-of-Jesus theologians burn in the fire kindled by historical criticism), and this reluctance was naturally accompanied by a diminution of interest in history as such. To this must be added Bultmann's cherished conviction that the occasion of faith is the preaching of the Word (which need not be attached too closely to a historical event, provided that it refers to it); and that in studying how this faith was transmitted we are studying what is most precious about the gospels; for, as Bultmann and others are fond of reminding us, these are not biographies or factual records, but kerygma.

Nevertheless, the form critics always allowed that their goal was to get back to the earliest tradition, even if they seldom in practice tried to take the last step back from the tradition to the event or saying that it enshrined or expressed. What is more, they admitted in principle that part of their job consisted in obtaining 'some idea of the purpose and technique of the redactor', and in fact the third (though much the shortest) of the three sections in Bultmann's *History of the Synoptic Tradition* was entitled 'The Editing of the Traditional Material'. To some extent, therefore, form criticism had paved the way for the fashion that succeeded it and which continues to dominate the scholarly study of the gospels.

Redaction Criticism

The form critics paid little attention to the broad sweep of the gospels and the powerful impact each of them makes when read as a united whole; and for this reason one is left wondering just how important their contribution to the field of gospel research has been and how it will finally be assessed when we are in a position to see it in its proper perspective. There remains something oddly myopic about their detailed scrutiny of individual passages in the gospels, and the Greek name for these 'pericopes' does in fact conjure up the image of a flat slab of pastry cut into tidy little rings ready for baking. They cut and carve rather than stitch and sew, and tend to regard the evangelist as little more than an inspired Autolycus, a picker-up of unconsidered pericopes. A reaction was bound to set in.

Set in it did, in the mid-1950's, with the arrival of redaction criticism. In some respects this name is unfortunate. A redactor is a compiler, building with other men's bricks, and the term does not usually suggest much original or creative thought. And since the whole thesis of the redaction critics is that the evangelists were more than mere compilers, it could be seriously misleading. On the other hand, it is clear that the evangelists *have* built with other men's bricks: none of the gospels was composed at a sitting, like most of St Paul's letters; and only St John's gospel could make any claim to be a carefully planned and constructed unity like the Letter to the Hebrews – and even this claim has been powerfully contested. As for the synoptic gospels, they were composed somewhat like the Pentateuch, by selecting and adapting already existing documents, many of which would have been written down only at the end of a longish period of oral transmission. Whoever gave the Pentateuch its final shape was a redactor in this sense; so were Matthew, Mark and Luke.

The practitioners of redaction criticism, with rare exceptions, work on the hypothesis of what is called the 'two-source theory'. This is one of the many hypotheses elaborated in the nineteenth century in answer to the famous synoptic problem, which is concerned with the relationship of the synoptic gospels with one another. Put rather baldly, the theory amounts to this: the earliest gospel to be written down was that of Mark; alongside Mark, independent of him, but containing a few passages stemming from a common tradition, is a hypothetical document, now lost, known as Q. The exact nature of this document is disputed, and since it is lost the disputes are unlikely ever to be definitively resolved. The most popular view is that Q was not a gospel but simply a random collection of sayings, unconnected by any narrative and strung together by means of rather arbitrary links, among them the occurrence of key-words or 'hook'-words. Mark's gospel and the hypothetical document Q, so the theory continues, were available to both Matthew and Luke, who took over and adapted the materials they contain. The explanation of the similarities between Matthew and Luke is that they made independent use of the two sources common to them both.

This solution of the synoptic problem is widely accepted by Protestant and Anglican scholars, but still hotly contested by a number of Catholic scholars, who feel that it does not do justice to the long-standing tradition of the priority of Matthew. However, there is no longer any 'official' Catholic answer to the synoptic problem, and those who reject the two-source theory do so because, for one reason or another, it appears to them to be an unsatisfactory solution. But there is no need to enter into this dispute here. The point to notice is that whereas the synoptic problem itself does not touch upon the aims and methods of the evangelists, redaction criticism is concerned with little else. Since, according to the hypothesis I have just outlined, it is obviously going to be easier to suggest reasons why Matthew and Luke, who had the text of Mark in front of them, chose to diverge from this tradition than it is to explain the purposes of Mark, whose sources can only be reconstructed hypothetically, it follows that redaction criticism has on the whole paid more attention to Matthew and Luke than it has to Mark. But Mark too built his gospel from already existing materials, and at least in some instances it may be possible to show that there were certain points he wanted to stress and certain ways in which he may have altered or adjusted the traditions he inherited.

As a example of redaction criticism we may take the story of the call of Levi and compare the accounts of Mark and Luke. The former is presumably the original version. Mk 2.13-17 falls into two distinct parts: a tiny vocation narrative and a pronouncement story. The link between the two parts is found in the words 'in his house'. The house is the house of Levi, the son of Alphaeus. (Alphaeus is evident-

36

ly an individual well known to whoever first recounted the story.) But in the pronouncement story, no stress at all is laid on the fact that it is Levi's house; the word 'house' is simply a link. Thus Levi's role as host is minimized; the real host, one feels, is Christ, whose call to sinners is basically an invitation to share in the table-fellowship of Jesus and his disciples. The point of the story is that by eating with tax-collectors and sinners Jesus was performing a shocking action, and he defended himself by an appeal to prophecy.

If we turn now to Luke's account we shall find that he has introduced some small but significant changes. In the first place, he has omitted the designation 'son of Alphaeus' which Mark, interested in this personage for his own sake, feels necessary to include (presumably to set him off from all the other Levis around at the time). Luke's interest in the story is different. For him, the man is a type of the Christian disciple, the follower of Christ. So he adds the words 'and he left everything'. That this is an addition which does not really fit in with the sequel to the story is shown by the fact that a line or two further on we find this same man laying on a lavish banquet for a large number of guests, and, curiously enough, Luke emphasizes this much more than his source does. For Mark, as we have seen, the word 'house' is simply a linking word.

So in the second part of Luke's account, the pronouncement story, we find this man who has just forsaken everything organizing an elaborate feast in Jesus' honour. Inconsistent, yes, but Luke evidently wants to stress that Jesus is the guest. It might be argued that he was the guest in Mark's account as well. True, but there he dominated the scene, and one gets the impression from Mark's account that even if 'in his house' seems to refer most naturally to Levi's own house, nevertheless Jesus is really the host, not the guest, and that the call at the end is an invitation he issues to share a meal with him. In Luke, on the contrary, the invitation has nothing to do with meals or table-fellowship. By adding the words 'to repentance', he turns what was originally a highly significant, broad-ranging invitation, displaying one of the most important features of the kingdom of God Jesus had come to proclaim, into a moral exhortation. The addition of these two words, 'to repentance', has separated the call from the meal. Luke saw Jesus' action of frequenting the company of sinners not as a sign that they were now welcome guests at his table, but as an indirect call to repentance. The same interpretation is manifest in the mercy parables in his fifteenth chapter. And in fact all three alterations are the product of concerns characteristic of Luke: (1) the stress on the disciple's need for renunciation; (2) the portrayal of Jesus as a guest; (3) the change from invitation to exhortation.

Another example: the Simon of Cyrene episode. Mark's interest in Simon arises largely from the fact that he was the father of Alexander and Rufus. The point of mentioning these names here (Mk 15.21) is probably that these two were well-known figures in the early Christian community and that they could testify to what their father had told them of his experience. Mark says that Simon was *compelled* (it is a strong word, meaning 'requisition' or 'press into service') to carry Jesus' cross. Luke uses a much milder word, which besides meaning 'impose', 'lay upon', can also mean 'entrust'; and he shows Simon following Jesus with the cross. The vocabulary Luke uses is the same as that used elsewhere in his gospel of the disciple who carries his cross behind Jesus (Lk 9.23). So Simon is no longer taken as the father of the witnesses Alexander and Rufus, whom Luke does not even mention, but as the type of Christian discipleship. Similarly the holy women who, in Mark's gospel, are named because they too can testify to the truth of the account that has been given of the Passion, have a very different role in Luke, where their attitude of quiet contemplation serves as a model for the Christian believer's response to the story that has just been told. 'And all his acquaintances and the women, who had followed him from Galilee stood at a distance and saw these things' (Lk 23.49). Throughout his account of the Passion, Luke is concerned to elicit the response of loyalty, grief, wonder and admiration from the Christian reader in a way that is demonstrably different from Mark, whose account is much starker, much more uncompromising than his.

The redaction critics are interested, then, in the dominating ideas and principles that provide the thrust behind each of the synoptic gospels and give each its characteristic flavour. It is true that much of the work done along these lines is subtle and difficult, and that the average reader is much more conscious of the similarities in the synoptics than of their differences. But after a time one becomes more responsive to Matthew's emphasis on the Church, on the Christian community, to Mark's central concern with the mystery of the Person of Christ, to Luke's particular interest in, say, the themes of salvation, discipleship and the Spirit, and to his tendency to file down some of the jagged edges that are still present in Mark and might offend the susceptibilities of less robust readers.

There are two dangers inherent in redaction criticism as it is currently practised. The first is that the two-source theory is not as secure as is commonly supposed and cannot bear the weight that is sometimes put upon it. The second danger is inseparable from the method as such. Its purpose, as we have seen, is to study the aims and techniques underlying the changes each evangelist had introduced into the traditional materials and thereby to arrive at some conclusion concerning his overriding interests. Some blocks of material he will introduce more or less as he has received them, others he will alter quite considerably. The net result is likely to be that certain passages will be more helpful than others to the redaction critic; some passages may indeed seem inconsistent with the writer's overall purpose, his 'theology' as it is often termed nowadays. None of the evangelists sets out deliberately to tamper with the tradition. They will want to express it as best they can and at the same time to underline the elements they regard as particularly important. So while they are prepared to adjust and trim their materials to serve this end, they are not prepared to carve them about indefinitely. The result is bound to be a certain inconsistency within the finished narrative.

It is this inconsistency that is responsible for the risk inherent in the method. For when I stumble across a word or phrase that does not fit in with my conception of what Luke is trying to say, then I can simply assert that it is part of an especially recalcitrant body of material which he is either unable or unwilling to adapt to his own scheme. On the other hand, anything that *does* fit in with my idea of his central purpose I can attribute without further ado to his own invention. The shadow cast over redaction criticism by this vicious circle can, I think, be successfuly circumvented, but in order to circumvent it one must first of all spot it.

CHAPTER 3

CHRIST OUR LORD AND THE APOSTLES

So far we have been concerned with the way in which scholars have approached the gospels since the onset of critical exegesis and with some of the techniques they have elaborated. We now turn to the gospel tradition itself, commencing with the first two stages of that tradition as outlined in the *Instructio de historica Evangeliorum veritate* quoted on pp. 12-15.

Christ our Lord

The gospels as we know them are the last fine flowering of a very complex process of growth and development, in which numerous factors were at work. At their source was the public career of Jesus of Nazareth, the personal impact he made upon his friends and followers, above all his extraordinary teaching, uncompromising and unforgettable. This is the first stage of the tradition.

Jesus belonged to a nation with a long history, keenly aware of its past and constantly seeking for new insights within its sacred writings. He lived at a time when his country was occupied by a foreign power, whose representatives had formed an uneasy alliance with the priestly aristocracy, the people's hereditary leaders. It was a time marked by sporadic revolts against the aggressors, revolts which, though ineffectual, kept the country in a constant state of tension. Jesus' message was far from political, but it had political overtones: ideas are dangerous, ideals even more so, and neither the Roman authorities nor the Jewish priests could be pleased with the implications of the ideas and the ideals of Jesus. In spite of mutual contempt and mistrust, they joined forces to bring about his downfall, and he was condemned to the most cruel and ignominious death of all, crucifixion. So after a brief and bewildering career he was put to death, nailed to a cross bearing the ironical inscription, *The King*

of the Jews. His friends had deserted him, and at least momentarily he was afraid that God had too. By any reasonable assessment his life had been a failure.

The gospels themselves furnish much of the information we have about contemporary Judaism, though they do so incidentally and almost casually. The precise relationship between the Sadducees and the priestly aristocracy, for instance, is still obscure, though it was clearly very close. In some ways Jesus was nearer to the Pharisees, who were less conservative than the Sadducees and much more interested in bringing religion to the people. The Jewish historian Josephys, pathetically anxious to defend his country's institutions to the uncomprehending Romans, tells us something, the learned Philo something more, about the nature and quality of contemporary Jewish beliefs. Besides the Pharisees and the Sadducees, Josephus names a third sect, the Essenes, not mentioned in the gospels, concerning whom we now have firsthand information.

Discoveries around the shores of the Dead Sea, dating from 1947, show that Jesus lived at a time when the apocalyptic expectations which had been building up over the preceding couple of centuries had already found some remarkable expressions. A number of especially ardent believers had chosen to cut themselves off from their fellowmen and to lead a secluded, monastic existence in some caves situated in what must surely be one of the most desolate regions of the earth. These, the so-called 'monks' of Qumrân, reflected constantly upon their national heritage and quietly awaited the coming of the kingdom of God. Like John the Baptist, they proposed to 'prepare for the coming of the Lord', but whereas John preached repentance thoughout Judaea and openly proclaimed the coming of the kingdom, the Essenes shrank from all contact with the masses and studied the Bible in meditative isolation.

Little can be said about Jesus' personality, for two reasons. On the one hand, the gospels evince scarcely more interest in his character and temperament than in the colour of his eyes. It is true that Jesus emerges as a most unusual man, strong and yet at the same time good and gentle, the most difficult combination of characteristics an imaginative writer can set himself to portray. (Think how differently we are affected by Prince Myshkin, whom Dostoyevsky certainly intended as a Christ-figure: though unquestionably a rounded character and no mere cardboard cut-out, he convinces largely because of his congenital weakness.) What is more, much can be learnt indirectly about Jesus' attitudes from his markedly unconventional habit of conversing easily and freely with women and children, as well as from his readiness to consort with social outcasts. But the gospels leave plenty of room for sentimental speculation, and if we could rid ourselves of all our preconceived ideas about Jesus and read, say, Matthew and Luke with fresh eyes, we should discover that Luke's Jesus is an altogether gentler and more immediately sympathetic figure than the stern, uncompromising, moral teacher we find in Matthew. Luke brings out the implications behind Jesus' message of forgiveness, but the point he is making is first and foremost a theological one.

This leads us to the second reason why it is hard to derive much direct information about Jesus' personality from the gospels: the whole gospel tradition is so deeply imbued with reflections on the *role* Christ plays in the Church that it becomes extraordinarily difficult, as Kähler, Wrede and the form critics have shown, to descry the lineaments of the historical Jesus beneath the patina superimposed upon the earliest traditions by the vibrant faith of the young Christian churches. And the task of removing this patina, though not perhaps as utterly impossible as it is often made out to be, is not one to be attempted here. Equally difficult is the job of reconstructing the historical outlines of Jesus' career, shrouded as they are, like his person, behind catechesis and kerygma.

Nevertheless, it was indeed Jesus of Nazareth whom the apostles proclaimed to be the Risen Lord, and there must have been something in his life, as well as in his death, that made it possible for them to do so. And certain features of his work stand out. 'He went about doing good and healing all that were oppressed by the devil, for God was with him'

(Acts 10.38). So he was a healer and an exorcist: no amount of demythologizing can altogether succeed in eliminating the marvellous from the gospel portrait, though it does seem as if the community felt free to embroider and extend the tradition of Jesus' wonderful cures and nature miracles in their presentation of him as the Risen Lord. More important, however, than the sheer extraordinariness of his deeds was the significance that he and those that witnessed his career would have attached to them. They were viewed as signs of the advent of the kingdom of God and the dawn of the Messianic age; and the one who performed them, strengthened by the power of the Spirit of God, was, it came to be inferred, the Messiah himself.

More is known for certain about the *content* of Jesus' message. The expression 'reign' or 'kingdom of God' had apocalyptic overtones. A new age was imminent, in which God would reclaim allegiance over the hearts of men. So the proclamation of the kingdom contained a command as well as a promise. The only reasonable response was *metanoia*, total conversion, best expressed in the parables of the pearl and the treasure in the field: nothing is too precious to sacrifice for the sake of obtaining this gift. And sacrifice was necessary: God offered his love and his mercy, but demanded absolute obedience in return. No written law could exhaust his demands, which constituted a perpetual and inescapable challenge. To those who met this challenge and submitted themselves to the Father's will, Jesus offered a share in the kingdom. So novel and bizarre was the exchange that it could only be expressed by paradox: through repetition, the beatitudes have become familiar, even trite, but we have only to reflect on them seriously to see how revolutionary they really are. Happy are the poor, the sad, the hungry and the persecuted; woe to the rich, the merry, the replete and the well-spoken of, for their eyes are too dim and their ears too dulled by these present delights for them to be able to see and hear the object of God's promise.

The very intransigence of Jesus' demands will have impressed the people with a sense of his authority. Unlike the rabbis, whom in other respects he resembled and from

44

whose teaching he had derived much, he did not merely set out to interpret the law; quite often he put his own teaching above it: 'You may have heard it said... but *I* say to you...' Jesus rejected the basic teaching of the Pharisees, carried over into later Judaism, that the will of God could be circumscribed by a written law. One who had observed all God's commandments, including the most important, from his youth had not yet attained perfection; 'Come, follow me'. And where the law made no sense it was simply set aside. The Pharisees' interpretation of the rules respecting the sabbath observance was, as it happened, considerably more liberal than that prevailing at Qumrân. But Jesus simply used their interpretation as an *argumentum ad hominem* to justify a course of action they condemned. As for the laws concerning ritual purification, Jesus clearly had no time for these at all, and his complete dismissal of the whole principle underlying such laws may be said to mark the true beginning of what is now known as secularization: for his words pierce the age old dam separating sacred and profane. 'Thus he declared all foods clean,' remarks St Mark (Mk 7.19), and we find St Paul making essentially the same point in one of his letters (1 Cor 8).

Jesus's freedom in regard to the conventions currently accepted in his own day was exhibited, of course, in his readiness to heal on the sabbath and to eat from contaminated vessels. But far more significant than the occasional breach of etiquette was his attitude towards women and children on the one hand and tax-collectors and sinners on the other. Women and children he treated with a sympathy and understanding remarkable in the society in which he moved; the hated tax-collectors and all those who, for one reason or another, had outlawed themselves from Jewish society by regularly breaking a code of law tacitly accepted by all 'decent' people received from him nothing but courtesy and respect. He was impatient with social barriers of this kind, embodying as they did the sort of moral censoriousness which 'good' people find hard to shake off (If the parable of the Pharisee and the Publican were taken seriously, the Sunday tabloids would soon go out of business).

Even so, Jesus did not come to condone sin but to offer sinners the merciful forgiveness of God. Frequenting, willingly and unhesitatingly, the company of social outcasts and sitting down to eat and drink with them, he made the same demands and held out the same promises to them as to all others. And it was his readiness to associate himself with these people that was the occasion of some of his most beautiful parables. The fifteenth chapter of Luke's gospel, one of the best loved in the Bible, opens like this: 'Now the tax collectors and sinners were all drawing near to hear him. And the Pharisees and the scribes murmured, saying, "This man receives sinners and eats with them." ' So the mercy parables (the Lost Sheep, the Widow's Drachma, the Prodigal Son) are first and foremost a defence of Jesus' own conduct. And his defence is astonishing: this, he says, is how God feels and thinks; I am exhibiting in my behaviour the mind and heart of God.

This quiet assurance that God saw and approved his actions horrified the religious leaders of the day, and it surely must have been one of the features of the authority whose source Jesus himself refused to name. To the believing Christian it is also one of the most convincing confirmations of his divinity, however shocking it seemed to his own contemporaries. But just as his miracles cannot be understood without reference to the reign of God which they inaugurated and whose nature they indicated, so the meals Jesus shared with sinners had an additional significance, underlined by Jesus in a further group of parables known as the 'banquet' parables. These show him eager to seat at God's table anybody and everybody prepared to accept his invitation. The response must be immediate – no excuse is accepted – and it must be total; the wedding garment symbolizes an unreserved compliance with God's demands. But once seated, the guests at this banquet participate in the table-fellowship of the kingdom of God, which was frequently portrayed in contemporary apocalyptic literature as a meal presided over by God himself.

This is the context, too, in which the Last Supper is to be understood. Jesus himself made this plain: 'I shall not drink again of the fruit of the vine until that day when I drink it new in the kingdom of God' (Mk 14.25). The Last Supper itself was not yet the eschatological banquet, but it was both the crown and climax of all those earlier meals in which Jesus had inaugurated a new table-fellowship and the model of those future meals in which Jesus' presence would be recalled and re-presented. The apostles are treated as the nucleus of the new Israel. They too sit upon thrones judging the twelve tribes, and now they are invited to partake of the cup of the New Covenant. Two of them had already been asked. 'Are you able to drink the cup that I drink?', and the real significance of their assent would shortly be brought home to them.

Jesus linked an announcement of his approaching death with the customary grace before and after the meal. He belonged to a society accustomed to read a religious significance into the Passover meal. So though the interpretation itself was new, it fitted easily enough into a ritual familiar to those with whom he shared his last meal. The idea of vicarious atonement was also part of their common tradition, and the paschal lamb was already linked, in the legend of the Binding of Isaac, with the notion of an expiatory sacrifice spontaneously and generously undertaken by a single individual. So Jesus, besides seeing his death as preparing the way for the coming of the kingdom in power and majesty (a vision closely associated for him with the mysterious figure of the Son of Man), also saw it as atoning in some way for the sins of the people.

Not that Jesus' self-questioning was over. The shrinking uncertainty of the Garden of Gethsemane gave way, at his trial, to a resounding confidence that he would soon be vindicated by God. But once on the Cross he hesitated again: 'My God, my God, why have you forsaken me?' He was spared none of the agonies, mental or physical, that can be suffered by the dying. And so he died and was buried and three days later rose again.

The Apostles

Jesus lived and died as a teacher. He was convinced that he

47

bore a message which, if accepted, would revolutionize the most important aspect of men's lives, their relationship with God. But if he had been nothing more than a great religious teacher, his message might well have died with him. For the power and authority of the Christian proclamation is not derived from Jesus' life and death but from his death and resurrection; and it was the conviction that he was risen from the dead that drove the apostles to preach him far and wide. Were it not for this assurance, which lent a new meaning to his words and works, it is unlikely that they would have made much headway. Indeed, all the indications are that they would have been too deeply discouraged even to start. In any case, they could have done little else except repeat Jesus' own promise of the coming of the kingdom: the content of their message would have been identical with his. And the central object of the Christian message is not the kingdom but the person of Christ: from being the proclaimer he had become the proclaimed.

Was he proclaimed straight away to be divine? This is a hard question to answer; though it was not long before the full implications of the Christian message became plain. Jesus' followers continued to believe in the one God worshipped by their Jewish forefathers, but they evidently had no difficulty (a fact remarkable enough to merit more comment than it generally receives) in reconciling this belief with the confession of Jesus as Lord. There can be no doubt that what made it possible for them to do this was the experience of the Resurrection.

From time to time in the course of his life a man may undergo an experience which can be properly be called revelatory: his whole outlook is altered, he sees his past in a different light, he will never be quite the same man again. Occasionally, most typically in the experience of falling in love, another person makes a dramatic entry into his life, and on such an occasion not merely is his own private history illuminated from within, but all his previous dealings with the other (however long or short a time they may have known one another) are suddenly shifted into bewilderingly unfamiliar patterns. Paths which had crossed now converge:

the world (which is always *my* world or *your* world) has been transformed.

Falling in love is no doubt a unique experience, but on a more mundane level we may become quite unexpectedly aware that we know another person intimately as never before. Our previous knowledge is shaped, quite compellingly, by something he has just done or said or by something we have just learned about him. All we knew before of his opinions and attitudes and character fits into place: the key has been found. So when St Luke describes how Jesus explained to the disciples on the road to Emmaus the secret of his life and death, he is indicating in a quite graphic way just what the resurrection meant to them. It helped them to see Jesus 'in a new light', but it was also the occasion of a faith which, in its total commitment, resembled nothing so much as the experience of falling in love. 'When Jesus rose,' said Scott Holland, 'his life rose with him'. If we grasp this truth we shall have understood what the gospels are all about.

Hard on the heels of the experience of the Resurrection, and powerfully reinforcing it, came the experience of the Holy Spirit. Not just from the Acts of the Apostles, but also from St Paul's letters, we get the impression of a vigour and a dynamism (the Greek word *dynamis* is frequently associated with the activity of the Spirit) whose effects were palpable. It was the Spirit who gave the apostles the courage and assurance they needed if they were continually to confront hostile audiences with their startling message, the Spirit who prepared the minds of both Jew and Gentile to receive it, the Spirit who directed the course taken by the apostolic preaching. The sense of the presence of the Spirit pervades all early Christian literature; and in a curious way this presence was felt to replace the physical presence of Jesus. Tertullian calls the Spirit 'the vicar of Christ', *'vicarius Christi'*. The Lord Jesus remained, but in a new way: it was in his name and through his Spirit that the gospel continued to be preached and wonders to be performed.

The conviction that they were still being taught by the Spirit persisted among the early Christians throughout apostolic times. Its disappearance marked the close of the apostolic age and the Christian revelation was complete. Not that St Paul could not distinguish between traditions received from the Lord and his own teaching: he could and did. But in adapting the words of Jesus and the stories about him to their own liturgical and catechetical needs, the early Christians were not in any way conscious of being disloyal to the message they had inherited. After the period of Jesus' own teaching came the second great period of the formation of the tradition, the tracing of which is the peculiar object of form criticism; and despite the many problems it entails, we cannot return to the sort of pre-critical immediacy which detected in every detail of the tradition concerning Jesus the stamp of his personality and the authentic echo of his voice. There is no need for the Catholic to be alarmed at this. The Church has never taught that revelation closed with the death of Jesus, but only with the death of the last apostle (a simple and time-honoured way of saying that the most important demarcation line is drawn after the completion of the canon of the New Testament). The formation of the canon raises further complex questions which cannot be dealt with here; but it would be silly to refuse to recognize an element of creativity in the Church's early handling of the tradition. The extent of this creativity had never been satisfactorily established. On the whole, Protestant scholars, at any rate on the Continent, are prepared to ascribe more to the invention of the early Christians than the majority of Catholics would wish to concede. But only a few wall-eyed conservatives maintain the strict word-for-word accuracy of all that is recorded in the gospels.

CHAPTER 4

THE EVANGELISTS

Eventually, nobody knows exactly when, the gospels were written down. Their final composition is traditionally ascribed to the four evangelists, Matthew, Mark, Luke and John, but the nature of the sources does not allow us any certainty about who the gospel writers were, what they were like, or even, except very approximately, when they lived. At any rate the traditions concerning Jesus were finally shaped into a coherent story which is neither biography nor memoir nor catechesis nor kerygma, but a mixture of all four blended together: in short, a gospel.

There are various theories about the pre-history of the gospel form. It may be that a sort of embryonic gospel, constructed roughly according to the pattern of the four that eventually gained full recognition by the Church, was already in existence before Mark's gospel was composed, probably between 60 and 65 A.D. Some scholars have claimed to be able to reconstruct such a gospel, or proto-gospel: it resembles Matthew, they say, more than Mark, and was composed in Aramaic. Others would maintain that the only really sustained episode to have circulated in written form before the composition of Mark's gospel was the passion-narrative: according to this view, a gospel is simply, in Martin Kähler's celebrated phrase, 'a passion-narrative with an extended introduction.' The sayings of Jesus may have been grouped together before this, but the principles of assembly will have been somewhat arbitrary. Some will have been stuck together because they shared a common form, like many of the wisdom sayings in the Sermon on the Mount; others because they represent Jesus in the same kind of situation, rebutting the accusations of the Pharisees or instructing his disciples of the kingdom. Still others will have been drawn together by the presence of the same word acting as a mnemonic device.

The hypothesis of a collection of sayings, existing along-side Mark's gospel and, like the latter, extensively drawn upon by Matthew and Luke, is, as we have seen, known as the two-source theory; and this is still the most widely held of the various solutions so far suggested for the so-called Synoptic Problem. Many scholars who tend on the whole to favour the two-source theory because of its simplicity and flexibility still find it necessary to postulate two further traditions, one known only to Matthew, the other only to Luke; and other scholars insist that allowance must be made for the possibility of oral as well as written sources. Still others, dissatisfied with that part of the theory which asserts that Mark's gospel was originally composed in the form we have it now, wish to replace it by a Proto-Mark. It was this earlier form of Mark, they say, which was known to Matthew and Luke. The Mark we possess is a slightly adapted version of it.

Thus modified, the two-source theory becomes not just flexible but flabby, with the result that some scholars have sagely and sceptically opted for an unpretentious but also, it must be admitted, largely unhelpful theory, known as the multiple-document theory. This is unsatisfactory as it stands because it fails to explain the remarkably close agreement in order and in substance between Mark and Matthew on the one hand and Mark and Luke on the other.

A satisfactory answer to the synoptic problem would clearly be of immense aid in determining the purposes of the individual evangelists, but it would go no distance at all in solving the problem of how and why a gospel came to be composed in the first place. The sources of the first gospel to be written down, whichever it happened to be, are irretrievably lost, except in so far as they can be reconstructed from the gospels themselves, and here, bereft of facts, we are compelled to resort to hypotheses. This is part of the more general difficulty that our knowledge of the whole of the period covered by the gospel tradition comes to us very largely from the gospels themselves. Something can be learnt of the intermediate stages from St Paul's letters and the Acts of the Apostles, but all enquiry into the origins of the traditions, as into their final arrangement and disposition, must begin and end with the four gospels. This means that even if we acknowledge in a general way that the source of the gospel tradition lies in the disciples' experience of Jesus, it is often not at all easy to say with any certainty when and why a particular theme came into prominence. Perhaps the actual composition of the first gospel represented a decisive moment in the developing consciousness of the Church: certain attitudes still clearly discernible within the pages of the gospels are incompatible with the structure and spirit of the gospels as a whole. But ideas and attitudes change only gradually, and the convictions that come to expression in the final draft of the four gospels may have taken root years earlier.

Eschatology

The most important and problematic area is that covered by the term 'eschatology'. Strictly speaking eschatology is simply 'that department of theology which is concerned with the "last things", with the state of the individual after death, and with the course of human history when the present order of things has been brought to a close' (*Hastings's Dictionary of the Bible*), in other words with what we call 'the next world' and 'the next life'. The Old Testament pictures life after death as a dim, witless existence in a shadowy, unreal place called Sheol, and (if we except the idea of resurrection) is innocent of any other concept that could be called eschatological in the strict sense.

But there is a derivative sense in which the term refers to expectations of a drastic change in the present order of things, and it is in this derivative sense that one may speak of notions like 'the day of Yahweh' or 'the kingdom of God' as eschatological. In the New Testament there are concepts which are clearly eschatological in the strict sense, such as the Parousia (the Second Coming of Christ) or bodily resurrection, and others which are only so if the less precise usage is admitted. Peter, for instance, preached at Pentecost of 'the last days' in which God promised to pour out his Spirit upon all flesh (Acts 2.17) in a way which implied that

53

the prophecy had already been fulfilled and that the last days had already come.

One of the great problems of gospel research is whether Jesus, like Peter at Pentecost, believed that the new aeon has arrived, or whether he thought of it as still to come. And if it was still to come, was it imminent or a long way off? Texts can be cited in favour of all these positions, though recently scholarly opinion has tended towards a view approximating that of Albert Schweitzer and Johannes Weiss: the urgency of Jesus' message is best explained by his belief in the imminent arrival of the kingdom of God. However this may be, it is clear from Paul's letters that the early Christians, Paul himself among them, were convinced that Christ would soon be returning in glory. And at a time when the prayer *Maranatha* ('Come, Lord Jesus') was on everybody's lips, it seems unlikely that anyone would have composed a lengthy and elaborate account of Jesus' earthly career. On this score alone the composition of the gospels probably belonged to a period when that conviction was on the wane, perhaps almost vanished. The gospels certainly retain traces of an earlier eschatology, one which the evangelists themselves no longer shared, but by the time the fourth gospel was composed there had been a serious attempt to rethink the problem and to eliminate most of the elements of apocalyptic expectation still to be found in the other three. In fact, traces of futuristic eschatology are still discernable in the fourth gospel, but they are notoriously hard to reconcile with the characteristically Johannine theology of 'eternal life', to which access is already given in this world by faith in Jesus.

One effect of eschatological hope is, in fact, to reduce interest in the past. In the excitement of an urgent and importunate hope the present is suffused with the future and history is forgotten. Apocalyptic dreams make time seem unreal: as soon as their magic fades the spring is released, the coils of time are stretched out and distinguished, and it makes sense once again to think in terms of past, present and future.

Part of the Q tradition (see p. 35) provides evidence of a

54

period in which the threat of Christ's imminent judgment no longer loomed as large as it did for the Thessalonians, so that the more restive and unruly spirits had to be warned that come Christ would, though there was no means of telling when. No doubt it was during this time of restlessness and uncertainty that the parables of the talents and of the wise and foolish virgins took their final shape: the bridegroom was delayed (Mt 25.5) and the man of property stayed away 'a long time' (Mt 25.19). In Matthew's gospel the long section stretching from 24.37 to 25.13 is basically a sharp reminder of the need for watchfulness in spite of the admitted uncertainty of the date of Christ's return: 'if that wicked servant says to himself, "My master is delayed" and begins to beat his fellow servants, and eats and drinks with the drunken, the master of that servant will come on a day when he does not expect him and at an hour he does not know' (Mt 24.48-50; cf. Lk 12.45f.).

So even during the period of the formation of the tradition, Christian catechists were confronted with the task of adapting the message of Jesus to the quite particular situation of a declining faith in the Parousia. But along with the growing suspicion that this was likely to be a long time off came the realization that Jesus was not only the Risen Lord whom they worshipped, but a man who lived at a particular time and in a particular place. Previously taken for granted, this seemingly obvious fact appeared sufficiently noteworthy to at least two of the evangelists (Matthew and Luke) to deserve some stressing. But though expressed in a different way by each, the awareness of the past as past was certainly a factor in the composition of all four gospels. In Luke, as we shall see, it took the form of a theology of the history of salvation; in John of a highly sophisticated theology of the Spirit.

The Person of Jesus

Right from the beginning, the Christian community acknowledged Jesus as Messiah and Lord. As Messiah, he answered the expectations of the Jews and fulfilled the Scriptures. As Lord, he was worshipped in the present and awaited in the future. 'Jesus is Messiah'; 'Jesus is Lord'. In one form or another, these primitive confessions of faith are scattered throughout the New Testament. Often they are simple and readily recognizable: 'because if you confess with your lips that Jesus is Lord and believe in your heart that God raised him from the dead, you will be saved' (Rom 10.9); 'Peter answered him, "You are the Christ"' (Mk 8.29). Sometimes they are skillfully elaborated in the form of hymns, such as the well-known Christological hymn in Philippians. But they are all two-sided; they all proclaim the identification of Jesus of Nazareth, the man who died, with the promised Messiah or the Risen Lord. Christianity cannot dispense with these confessions of faith: it can adapt and develop them, build them into creeds, draw out their implications in language mystical or philosophical, but the fundamental affirmation remains the same.

In a sense, therefore, the modern distinction between the historical Jesus and the kerygmatic Christ was acknowledged and overcome long before it presented itself as a difficult speculative problem. Paul, it is true, pays little attention to the life and teaching of Jesus, and John is so busy showing the human as divine that it is tempting to regard the humanity of Jesus as undervalued in the fourth gospel. But neither loses sight of the basic faith in the identity of the Christ they proclaim with the Jesus of history. The Johannine writings in particular never tire of affirming 'the coming of Jesus Christ in the flesh' (2 Jn 7), for 'every spirit which confesses that Jesus Christ has come in the flesh' (1 Jn 4.2) is of God.

Nevertheless, some tension may have developed between the two aspects of Christ's person held together in these early confessions. His humanity continued to be displayed, clearly and unmistakably, in the story of his passion and death. But the hesitancy with which he claimed Messianic honours was undoubtedly underplayed by Christian preachers; and as for his lordship and divinity, any exaggerated emphasis on these will have flourished in the soil of the miracle tradition. Dominated by an intense awareness of his spiritual presence and authority, the early Christians attributed to the earthly Jesus powers which he received through his resurrection. Originally, no doubt, this was done deliberately, in order to point a moral or elucidate some principle of the faith.

Matthew's version of the story of the walking on the sea is a good example of this. C.H. Dodd has argued that even in the earlier version of Mark this story may be a resurrection-appearance transferred subsequently to its present position. ('The Appearances of the Risen Christ: An Essay in Form-Criticism of the Gospels', *More New Testament Studies* (1968) pp. 102-133). But whereas Mark concludes with a reference to the disciples' bewilderment, Matthew ends with an act of adoration which is certainly out of place at this point of Jesus' career: 'And those in the boat worshipped him, saying, "Truly, you are the son of God" ' (Mt 14.33). This cannot be easily reconciled with the earliest christology according to which Jesus was 'designated Son of God in power according to the Spirit of holiness by his resurrection from the dead' (Rom 1.4).

So the memory of a real man, beset by the weaknesses of ordinary humanity, had clouded over. Its place had been partly taken by the portrait of a man endowed with certain superhuman qualities, a portrait destined to endure. The tradition of Jesus' refusal to dazzle his contemporaries with signs and wonders was not lost, but it was obscured and the result was that the balance of the confession 'Jesus is Lord' was destroyed. Mark, as we shall see, used the device of the Messianic secret in an attempt to restore it.

The singularity of the gospel form is that it enables the divinity and humanity of Jesus to emerge in and through the story of his life and death. The traditions concerning him were not just strung together like beads on a string, as K.L. Schmidt, one of the early form critics, would have it, but composed as a continuous narrative. If generations of Christians have been misled into thinking of the gospels as biographies, or at any rate as quarries from which materials for a life of Jesus could be hewn, this is because they are set down in story form. Some years ago, swimming strongly against the tide of critical opinion, Professor C.F.D. Moule

57

argued that the gospels 'were in intention less interpretation, liturgy and theology than narrative statement' (*The Phenomenon of the New Testament* (1967), p. 100f.). His own view is that 'at the time when the gospels were being written and first used, the Church was well aware of a distinction between "the Jesus of history" and "the Christ of faith"; and that in so far as the gospels were used in Christian worship they filled a place broadly comparable to the narrative parts of the Hebrew Scriptures in the Synagogue, as the historical background against which the interpretative writings might be read' (p. 101). In some recent work on the gospels he detected and deprecated 'any implication of failure, in the primitive Christian community, to realize that there was some distinction in some sense – however impossible it was to draw it in practice – between "history" and "interpretation" ' (p. 102).

This opinion coheres with Dodd's view that the outline of the first gospel (Mark) was kerygmatic, and in fact Moule holds the purpose of the gospels to be closer to apologetic than to catechesis, that is to say directed more to unbelievers than to believers. There is certainly something to be said for this view, although it would be odd if so much undoubtedly catechetical material were collected and reordered to serve another purpose altogether. Form criticism was beamed almost exclusively, as we have seen, upon the period following the constitution of the Church and preceding the composition of the gospels. It was much more interested in the individual pericopes than in their total organization within the framework of a continuous narrative. But as Moule realized, the form of the gospels is itself a fact of some importance. Rendered possible by the weakening of eschatological expectation, it presented certain practical problems which each of the evangelists solved in his own way. This requires a word of explanation.

Looking back upon the traditions they had inherited concerning Jesus' life and teaching, for the most part isolated episodes given a point relevant to the situation of the community, the Christians of the second half of the first century saw Jesus not just as their present Lord and future Judge, but as a historical figure belonging, in some sense, to the past. The identification of Jesus as Lord had always been the touchstone of loyalty to the Christian faith; but the new view of him as a real historical personage required, or at least facilitated, an extended narrative of a kind hitherto confined to the story of the passion. Not that this presented any *speculative* problems: occasional sayings and miracles, instead of being transmitted in the form in which they were first told, had long been subjected to subtle forces designed to adapt them to the religious needs of the community, whether liturgical or catechetic; so there was no difficulty in principle about doing the same with a more protracted narrative. Nevertheless the large-scale narrative presented certain difficulties which the redactor (if one may be permitted to employ this rather colourless term) had either to solve or to circumvent.

A simple example: was the earthly Jesus to be referred to as 'Lord' within the context of the gospel story? Mark is shy of using the title (except in the vocative, where it has no special significance); Matthew employs it regularly; while Luke appears to use it only when he wants to stress the present bearing of the story he is recounting upon the lives of his readers. Again, was Jesus to be portrayed as offering salvation to all mankind or as confining his personal mission to Israel (historically much the more probable alternative)? Here it is Luke who is particularly cautious: although ready to drop hints indicating the universality of Jesus' mission, in general he suggests that the Christian message was not preached to the Gentiles until well after the Resurrection. Matthew's position is much more difficult to summarize because of the complexity of the tradition on which he drew, but he too seems to hold back the account of a universal mission until after the Resurrection. More important still is the question of the titles of Jesus, some of which present very knotty problems indeed to the exegete. Did he or did he not think of himself during his earthly career as 'Messiah', 'Son of Man', 'Son of God'? It goes without saying that the evangelists themselves believed that all these glorious titles were his by right, and no doubt found them in their sources. But was it not a little odd, a little difficult, to ascribe them to him in the midst of his earthly career? Problems like these obliged the evangelists to make certain options and prevented them from becoming mere compilers. Much of the art of redaction criticism lies in discerning their answers and in guessing why they answered as they did.

This is not the place to enter into a detailed discussion of the problems confronting the evangelists, but it is perhaps worth saying a word or two more on the implications for theology of the gospel form itself. Ernst Käsemann, who in 1954 proposed reopening the quest of the historical Jesus, rightly points out, in his reply to Bultmann's repudiation of his suggestion, that even John, much of whose material is of doubtful historicity, couches his theology in gospel form and inserts the central revelation within the traditional framework of the public life and the Easter mysteries. The fact that he does so shows his keen awareness that the best way to authenticate his message is to attribute it to Jesus himself: the context in which the revelation is found is all-important. 'This process', adds Käsemann, 'is therefore of the greatest significance because it enables us to acquire a right understanding of the Synoptists as being composers of gospels and not merely the gatherers of certain material which happened to be circulating at the time. Doubtless they are dominated by the interests of kerygma. But they express this in the form of gospels, which are essentially *not* preaching but reporting' (*New Testament Questions of Today* (1969), p. 49).

There is a further point to be made, one neglected by the majority of modern exegetes. Käsemann does not go far enough. The gospel form is not merely significant in itself but it affects the whole character of the message it contains. Dennis Nineham has shown how unlikely it is that the sequence of Mark's gospel reproduces at all accurately the order of events in Jesus' ministry; he illustrates his argument from the fact that all the episodes which take place in Jerusalem are bundled together towards the end of the gospel, giving the impression that Jesus paid only one visit to the capital, and this in order to face arrest and condemnation. It is highly likely that some of the incidents described here took place on earlier visits, not recorded by the evangelist. Then Nineham goes on:

> When we remember that many of the stories reached St Mark without any indication of the time or place at which they occured, we shall learn not to place on Mark's order a weight it was never intended to bear, and our question about each incident will be: 'what is the significance of St Mark's having placed it here *in his Gospel?*' not: 'what is the significance of its having happened at this point *in Our Lord's ministry?*' J.H. Ropes makes the point admirably when he writes: 'The form of the Gospel of Mark is, to be sure, that of narrative, but the important question is not of its form, but of its purpose; and that is theological' (*Saint Mark* (1963), p. 36f.).

But is this distinction between form and purpose valid? Can we assume so lightly that the continuous narrative in which Jesus' life and teaching are framed is an accidental irrelevance? Would a series of disconnected vignettes have had the same force or carried the same message? Would it have been a gospel at all? Surely the sheer fact that the gospels are composed in story form furnishes us with a key to their interpretation which many modern exegetes are inclined to toss onto a scrap-heap along with the lumber left over from the nineteenth century quest of the historical Jesus? This point is valid irrespective of the historical accuracy of the framework provided. A picaresque novel, for instance, which consists of a number of largely disjointed episodes displaying various facets of the hero's character, is essentially different from a book of short stories all figuring the same central character – Chesterton's Father Brown, for instance, or Somerset Maugham's Ashenden. In the novel there is always some movement and progression. At the end of Fielding's novel *Tom Jones,* the hero is a more mature personage than when we first met him: not merely does the reader know him better but he knows himself better.

There is a similar kind of development in the gospels.

61

Mark, for instance, presents his gospel in two successive stages in which the episode of Peter's confession at Caesarea Philippi acts as a kind of pivot. To ignore this structure or to leave it out of account is to fail to do justice to what, for a reader without religious or scholarly prejudice, is one of the gospel's most obvious features. The change of pace after Peter's confession and the growing sense of inevitability conveyed by the evangelist are just as much part of what he is trying to tell us as, say, the notion of the Messianic secret. We speak glibly of the picture of Jesus to be found in the gospels whilst forgetting sometimes that it is a *moving* picture.

How should these observations affect the interpretation of the gospels? Well, they should warn us that they are not just like Byzantine mosaics, coloured pebbles assembled to form a static portrait. We are entitled to speak of a progressive revelation in Mark's gospel. How far, though, is this historically accurate? Is it possible to say that Jesus revealed himself first as the Messiah and then as the Son of God? These are the sort of questions which delve below the surface of the gospels and which cannot in the nature of the case be answered directly.

We can attempt, of course, to answer them *indirectly,* and it can be argued on other grounds that it was only when Jesus' preaching of the kingdom failed to make any significant impact that he came to realize that success would only come with his death. But the evangelists are not interested in Jesus' developing awareness of the conditions of his mission, only in the general meaning of his career on earth for Israel and the Church. Part of the meaning, though, lies in the conjunction of the Passion narrative with the originally independent traditions of Jesus' teaching and miracles. The Jesus about to go to his death is someone we know, and we know him both from what he has said and from what he had done. The Passion narratives would lose much of their dramatic power if the central figure appeared on the scene for the first time, if he was not already familiar to us as a man who had preached total submission to the will of God and unhesitating forgiveness of one's enemies, who had performed miracles for others while consistently refusing to employ spectacular or flamboyant means of getting his message across.

CHAPTER 5

THE SYNOPTIC GOSPELS

Whole books have been written and continue to be written upon the theology of each of the synoptic gospels, upon their central purposes and individual concerns. No attempt will be made in this chapter to give a comprehensive survey of the results of redaction criticism. We shall simply single out a few important ideas in the hope of demonstrating the fruitfulness of this approach.

Mark and the 'Messianic Secret'

The term 'Messianic secret' was introduced into New Testament scholarship early this century by William Wrede, lonely pioneer of redaction criticism (*Das Messiasgeheimnis,* 1901) and all subsequent commentators have been compelled to take up some position in its regard. Wrede draws attention to Jesus' habit of enjoining silence upon all around him, including the demons and those he has cured. He teaches the crowd concerning the kingdom, and yet, when it comes to explaining his teaching, he withdraws to a private spot with his disciples so that no one else can benefit from the full revelation. He explains to them that he uses parables when teaching 'those outside' in order that 'they may see but not perceive, hear but not understand' (Mk 4.12), a curious motive, to say the least. And even the disciples notoriously fail to profit from the special explanations of which they are the beneficiaries. They, like the Pharisees and Jesus' kinsfolk, display an extraordinary obtuseness when it comes to grasping the main burden of his message.

No satisfactory *historical* explanation of these data has ever been given. Jesus' obsessive secretiveness just does not make sense. How could he hope to keep his miracles hidden? Having performed them in full view of everybody, he could not seriously expect that all the witnesses would refrain from talking about what they had seen. In fact, Mark himself admits that 'the more he charged them, the more zealously they proclaimed it' (7.36). As for the demons, they spoke out loud and clear *before* being told to keep quiet, and there is nothing to suggest that what they said was for Jesus' ears alone. Equally implausible is the assertion that the disciples, unlike everyone else, were warned in detail of Jesus' approaching passion and resurrection. For in that case, how was it that they were so shaken and suprised by these events when they came, so slow to understand?

A common explanation of these difficulties, one favoured by many commentators both before and after Wrede, is that our Lord was reluctant to give any grounds for misinterpreting his claims in a crudely political sense. But there is not the slightest support for this explanation in the pages of the gospel itself; and in any case, as Wrede says, surely Jesus could easily have guarded against such misunderstandings by spelling out, carefully, patiently and precisely, the true significance of his mission and by correcting mistakes as they arose?

Wrede finds the clue to this puzzle at the heart of the puzzle itself: 'he charged them to tell no one what they had seen, until the Son of man should have risen from the dead' (Mk 9.9). This sentence, he believes, informs us not about what actually occurred but about Mark's own attempt to make sense of conflicting traditions about Jesus: on the one hand he is portrayed as Messiah even during his lifetime, and on the other hand the basis for conferring this title on him is not to be found in anything he did before his death, but in his resurrection. The Messianic secret (which Wrede regards as pre-Marcan) is designed to explain why Jesus was not seen in his true glory until after he had risen from the dead. This was no accident: he himself had enjoined secrecy, since he was reluctant to be known as Messiah while he was still alive. Mark, according to Wrede, made this explanation his own and imposed it upon the traditions he had taken over, all of which were permeated with an unquestioning faith in Jesus' Messiahship.

Wrede assumed that no one had ever thought of Jesus as Messiah until after the Resurrection and that Jesus never in fact made any claim to messianic status. This view was adopted and defended by Bultmann, who took the argument a stage further. Wrede held that the Messianic secret was already part of the tradition, and that Mark simply extended it systematically to cover all the pre-passion material. No, says Bultmann, it was Mark who *invented* the Messianic secret; and a later writer, H.J. Ebeling, carrying the principles of form criticism even further, argued that the oral tradition on which Mark drew had no interest in presenting an accurate historical picture of Jesus: it had always been concerned with Jesus as seen through the eyes of a believer not as a figure of history (*Das Messiasgeheimnis und die Botschaft des Marcus-Evangelisten*, 1939).

In fact, the Messianic secret is *not* exclusively Marcan; it is found in Matthew's gospel in a passage derived from another source (Mt 9.27-31). Elsewhere, Matthew transposes the theme when he shows Jesus' deliberate evasion of public acclaim (Mt 12.27-31; 14.13 – 16.12); and John too, as we shall see, attributes to the utterances of the earthly Jesus a kind of systematic ambiguity to which the Holy Spirit alone has the key. 'Thus the common tradition underlying the gospels shows Jesus not merely as a Messiah who was in fact unknown, but as one who himself chose to conceal his identity' (X. Léon-Dufour, *The Gospels and the Jesus of History* (1968), p. 233).

Wrede was wrong to assume that there was ever a Jesus tradition free from Messianic elements. The Jewish-Christian community saw its master as Messiah right from the start, so there was never any question of having to reconcile two divergent interpretations of the tradition. Observing this, Ebeling was led to conclude that there was really no secrecy theory at all in Mark's gospel: the real purpose of the command to be silent was, he thought, to impress the reader with the profundity of the mystery which it was his privilege as a Christian to share. But this explanation is too subtle and far-fetched.

The Messianic secret did have a function, but it is not

that proposed by Wrede. Mark, far from imposing a theory upon his material, was concerned to underline its true nature: it portrayed Jesus in the light of the Resurrection, it was christological right from the beginning. The verse Wrede makes the cornerstone of his theory, Mk 9.9 (quoted above), expresses Mark's own insight that a proper understanding of Jesus' true nature was impossible until the resurrection had taken place. Starting from this realization, Mark (or his predecessor) then inferred that misunderstanding was inevitable, even necessary.

If there was a single block of the tradition that was *not* imbued with the bright hues of the Resurrection, this was the Passion narrative. Here was a man who foresaw his own death, certainly, but who, in the course of those last long days, performed none of the miracles and uttered few of the calmly authoritative sayings that marked his public life. His confident affirmation of his Messiahship before the Sanhedrin may have been included in the tradition (though probably the more tentative and discreet assent recorded by Matthew is the older and more original version here), but it was a claim which, because of the circumstances in which it was made, could not be misinterpreted. Mark saw that the true Christ was the suffering Christ. And this insight has controlled his treatment and organization of the stories of the teacher and wonderworker who figures in the remainder of the tradition.

Accordingly, he built up the (no doubt authentic) tradition of the incomprehension of Jesus' disciples into a coherent theory of the Messianic secret. This is particularly clear in the sequence to the Caesarea Philippi episode. With considerable dramatic skill, the evangelist shows how incomplete Peter's understanding of Jesus' Messiahship really was. Peter jibbed at the idea that glory must be preceded by suffering, that Jesus could not take on the role of the Son of Man and come in power to judge the world until he had undergone an ignominious death. And the effect of Jesus' reply was not just to reassure the faithful that he went knowingly and willingly to his death, but to show that an understanding of his Messiahship depended upon the Passion.

The Passion is at the heart of this text. The command to silence leads up to it; it is the content of the open teaching; the misunderstanding is disclosed in its presence. Wrede was right to find in Jesus' Passion predictions the clue to the Messianic secret, but he read the clue wrongly. The centre of the evangelist's concern is not the Resurrection (though this is evidently presupposed) but the Passion.

So Mark sees Jesus imposing secrecy upon the bystanders and cloaking his own teaching in parables for basically the same reason. Without the Cross, neither his actions nor his words can be properly understood. Mark's problem is that he is working with traditions from which the Passion motif is relatively absent, and which proclaim the authority of Jesus apart from the Cross.

> In order to appropriate these traditions in a positive fashion and to bring them in harmony with the paradoxical revelation of the authority of Jesus through his passion and death, Mark adds these detaining corrections which hold back the climax until the cross is reached and point constantly towards it. This intention of the Evangelist corresponds also to the phenomenon of misunderstanding of the disciples which accompanies the passion prophecies and the way of Jesus to the cross in the second part of the gospel. He shows how Jesus is *not* to be understood – apart from suffering and death; but he also shows thereby *how* Jesus can be understood – in suffering and death, beneath the cross (15.39), and in the discipleship of suffering in which the paradox of God's action through Jesus is continued in the life of Christians (8.27-33). ...Mark has brought the problem of understanding within the embrace of the *theologia crucis*. That may well be the greatest achievement of Mark as theologian (H-D. Knigge, 'The Meaning of Mark' *Interpretation* 22 (1968) p. 70).

This has its significance for the Christian *qua* Christian. Discipleship also involves suffering. Incomprehension is a major theme of Mark's gospel, one which culminates in the flight of Jesus' disciples after his arrest. Mark punctuates the first half of the pre-Passion material (up to Caesarea Philippi) with reports on the failure of various groups of men to understand his message; the second half is dominated by his disciples' misunderstanding of his invitation to take up their cross and follow him. The paradox of the gospel is the nature of its good news. But of course to a Church struggling against persecution and difficulty the spectacular news of Jesus' career as a wonder-worker was not unambiguously good news. 'He who finds his life [i.e. his self] will lose it, and he who loses his life for my sake will find it' (Mt 10.39). This saying, given by Matthew in an earlier form, was at the heart of Jesus' teaching. Mark shows how it is also the key to his own conduct on earth and must be accepted unreservedly by his followers. If they do so they will be living and dying for Jesus' sake 'and for the sake of the gospel' (Mark's contribution to the logion: 8.35). For in the last analysis Mark identifies the message with the messenger, the gospel with the person of Jesus.

Luke and Salvation History
The most striking difference between Luke and the other evangelists is that his work is twice as long as theirs. Scholars are agreed that Luke planned to write two books from the outset. The structural and thematic links between the Book of Acts and the third gospel are clearly marked and numerous, though they differ widely in style, approach and subject-matter. Luke underlines his intention of making a fresh start simply and effectively by repeating his account of the Ascension at the beginning of his second book.

The gospel is concerned with the life and death of Jesus, the Acts with the period following his final departure from the world, the era, that is, of the early growth of the Church, in which the apostles, the witnesses of Jesus' resurrection, spread the good news far and wide, 'even to the ends of the earth' (Acts 1.8). They are assisted in this task by the Holy Spirit, who is at one point associated directly with their work of attesting to the basic truths of the Christian proclamation: 'And we are witnesses to these things,' Peter tells the Jewish council, 'and so is the Holy Spirit whom God had given to those who obey him' (Acts 5.32). So prominent a role does the Holy Spirit play in Luke's second book that it has been named 'the Gospel of the Spirit' – not a good title, in fact, since it blurs the real meaning of the word 'gospel', but a suggestive one nonetheless, since it is clear that for Luke the era of the Church is also in a special sense the era of the Spirit and since he is in fact the only one of the synoptics to picture Christ as bestowing the Spirit on the apostles (Lk 24.49, to be read along with Acts 1.4-5).

However, the Spirit was already active during the lifetime of Jesus, who was conceived through his special intervention (Lk 1.35) and received him in a particular manner at his baptism (Lk 3.22). Jesus' baptism was his first public act, and it has a special significance for Luke in that it marks the beginning of the period of Jesus' life and teaching to which the apostles were called upon to give witness. This is 'the word which was proclaimed throughout all Judaea, beginning from Galilee after the baptism which John preached: how God anointed Jesus of Nazareth with the Holy Spirit and with power: how he went about doing good and healing all that were oppressed by the devil, for God was with him. And we are witnesses to all that he did both in the country of the Jews and in Jerusalem' (Acts 10.37-39). The anointing mentioned here also figures in another key-episode in Luke's gospel, in which Jesus, having returned from his long fast in the desert 'in the power of the Spirit', stood up to read the lesson in the synagogue at Nazareth. 'The Spirit of the Lord, he read, 'is upon me, because he has anointed me to preach good news [= to spread the gospel] to the poor... Today this scripture has been fulfilled in your hearing' (Lk 4.18-21). This episode is peculiar to Luke and has a programmatic function in his gospel. Here it is sufficient to stress that Jesus' life, like his birth, was overshadowed by the Spirit until, at his resurrection and ascension, he finally received the Spirit for transmission to others: 'Being therefore exalted at the right hand of God, and having received from the Father the promise of the Holy Spirit, he has poured out this which you see and hear' (Acts 2.33).

It is clear, then, that for Luke the Ascension marked a turning-point in the activity of the Spirit, who from being closely, almost exclusively, associated with Jesus' person and preaching, became available, as it were, to all mankind, not as a principle of inner sanctification but as a powerful force invariably accompanying the preaching of the gospel. All who, through the mediation of the Church, learn to acknowledge the truth of the gospel have a share in the fruits of the Spirit. Not that their relationship with the Spirit is as full or as deep as that of Jesus, for he receives him in virtue of his divine sonship (cf. Lk 3.22), whereas for the Christian the Spirit is 'the promise of the Father' (Lk 24.49; Acts 1.4), and is, in a special sense, the object of his prayer (Lk 11.3, to be compared with Mt 7.11).

But if the distinction between Luke's two books may be drawn according to the role accorded to the Spirit in each, it remains true that the Spirit was active even before the coming of Christ: he it was who spoke through the prophets (cf. Acts 28.25). The last of the prophets was John the Baptist, who 'grew and became strong in spirit' (Lk 1.80), and who, at his naming ceremony, was himself the object of the remarkable prophecy of the *Benedictus*: 'And you, child, will be called the prophet of the Most High; for you will go before the Lord to prepare his ways' (Lk 1.76). The mission of Jesus, followed by the era of the Church, is preceded by the era of prophecy. In each of these periods the role of the Spirit is fundamental.

The Spirit, then, is everywhere is the Lucan writings, but so of course is Jesus Christ, who continues to make his presence felt to the apostles, especially Peter and Paul, even after his death. The clue to *how* he does so is to be found in the expression 'the Spirit of Jesus'. As well as being the protagonist of the gospel, Jesus is the object of both prophecy and proclamation. The 'Scriptures' foretell his coming, the gospel describes his coming, and the kerygma of the Acts proclaims his coming to both Jew and Gentile, showing at the same time how it fulfils the Scriptures (as Jesus himself was the first to do, on the way to Emmaus).

This tripartite division is one of the main themes of H.

Conzelmann's book, *The Theology of St Luke* (1960). Though frequently challenged, his contention that behind Luke's work it is possible to detect a fairly elementary theology of salvation history has much to be said for it. He attaches great weight to Lk 16.16: 'The law and the prophets were until John; since then the good news of the kingdom of God is preached.' Unlike Matthew, whose version is generally agreed to be the earlier, Luke ranges John the Baptist on the side of the prophets, and structures his gospel accordingly: 'The coming of John does not mean that the kingdom is at hand, but that the time for preaching the kingdom had come' (Conzelmann, *op. cit.* p. 112). Since he appears only in the role of prophet, it is Jesus himself who has the task of bringing the good news of the kingdom to Israel. But it is in virtue of his anointing by the Spirit that he is enabled to do this, just as after his death it is through the Spirit that 'the things which have been accomplished among us' (Acts 1.1) are rendered accessible to others. The Scriptures are absorbed into the events of Jesus' life and death, and his life and death are absorbed into the kerygma, thus enabling him to exercise his lordship over all mankind.

The same triple structure is discernible in another way. The story of Israel, from the books of Kings onwards, is one of a gradually diminishing authority and power. First the Davidic kingdom was shorn of its external dominions, then split into two parts, each with its own capital. In 721 Samaria, the capital of the Northern kingdom, fell to the might of Assyria, and in 587 Jerusalem too was finally overwhelmed, and there began the long Babylonian captivity. It would be a very long time before the Jews regained any real independence.

Now Luke, although no Jew himself, is very much aware that in the person of Jesus the promises made to Israel have been fulfilled. The *Nunc Dimittis* spoken by Simeon places the tiny baby, astonishingly, within the perspective of the history of Israel and of the surrounding peoples: 'for mine eyes have seen thy salvation, which thou hast prepared in the presence of all peoples, a light for revelation to the Gentiles and for glory to thy people Israel' (Lk 2.30-32).

There is a sense, indeed, in which Jesus *was* Israel, the stump of Jesse, the sole representative of that Remnant of which Isaiah had spoken darkly eight centuries before. Luke lays great stress on the importance of the city of Jerusalem, where all prophets must die (Lk 13.33), and the main function of the great journey narrative (Lk 9.51-19.28) is to show Jesus turning his steps towards Jerusalem, where the central mystery of salvation – his passion, death and resurrection – would be enacted and where the infant Church would be born.

Starting from the narrow confines of a single room, the message of the gospel would be preached first in the city of Jerusalem, then in the territory of Judaea, afterwards in Samaria and eventually well beyond the frontiers of the Davidic empire, 'even to the ends of the earth' (Acts 1.8). So the decline of the material fortunes of Israel in the Old Covenant is matched by the gradual spread of the gospel of the New Covenant. Christianity was to reach Rome only after the evangelization of what used to be the divided kingdoms of Israel and Judah, and the slight artificiality of this scheme does nothing to detract from its programmatic importance. The triple division we have already considered had a historical significance as well as a theological one, and the Lucan writings probably have a better claim to the title of 'salvation history' than any of the other books of the New Testament. Unfortunately, Israel rejected the proffered salvation: 'Let it be known to you then that the salvation of God has been sent to the Gentiles; they will listen' (Acts 28,28).

Matthew and the New Law

The original gospel, if one may speak in this rather loose way of Mark or Proto-Mark, was kerygmatic: it was intended not just to nourish the faith of believers, but to elicit the response of faith from unbelievers. In Matthew and Luke the kerygmatic character is chiefly preserved in the gospel form. Their interest has shifted from the central mystery of the person of Christ to aspects of this mystery which were directly relevant to their own situation. In Luke this means an overriding emphasis on salvation-history; in Matthew's gospel proclamation seems somehow to be swallowed up in teaching, or perhaps it would be more accurate to say that proclamation is conceived as teaching.

In the first place, there is no clear distinction in Matthew between the use of the verbs '*kerussein*' (proclaim) and '*didaskein*' (teach). It is no doubt true that the distinction is not altogether obvious in Mark either, but Mark is more interested in the fact that Jesus is a teacher than in the details of his doctrine: what counts for him is the authority, not the content of his teaching, except in so far as he identifies Jesus himself with his own message. Where Matthew sets the two terms together (4.27; 9.33; 11.1), he does so because for him the challenge implicit in the proclamation is embodied in the ethical teaching. And since it is no longer possible to distinguish, as it is in Mark's gospel, between moral exhortation and kerygmatic proclamation, it follows that Matthew must be addressing himself primarily to a community whose response to the challenge of the gospel takes the very concrete form of obedience to the exigencies of the new law: the earliest Christian confession consisted, as we saw, in a simple affirmation of the lordship of Jesus of Nazareth. Matthew's gospel is full of instances which show how unreservedly the Christian must put his faith in his Lord (we have already considered his handling of the episode of the walking on the waters); but real faith, as he insists, must issue in works: 'Not every one who says to me, "Lord, Lord" shall enter the kingdom of heaven, but he who does the will of my Father who is in heaven' (Mt 7.21).

In Matthew's adaptation of the kingdom theme we see clearly how he manages to combine what was originally an eschatological concept with an ethical ideal. In three passages, all secondary and redactional in character (4.23; 9.35; 24.14), he employs the curious phrase 'the gospel of the kingdom'. In Mark, the gospel is Christ and it is arguable that the mystery of the kingdom is Christ also. But in Matthew 'the gospel of the kingdom' is a *formula*, and the kingdom has become something that is taught, as in the equivalent expression 'word of the kingdom' (13.19). And what is taught is no longer the central mystery of the person of Christ, but an ethical programme of some complexity. It is significant that in the all-important explanation of the parables, where Mark reads the singular ('the mystery of the kingdom'), Matthew has the plural ('the secrets of the kingdom', 13.10).

Matthew alone of all the evangelists records the remarkable aphorism, 'every clerk who has become a disciple [by being instructed] in the kingdom of heaven is like a householder who brings out of his treasure new things and old' (13.52). It has been suggested (by C.F.D. Moule, *The Birth of the New Testament*, 1962, p. 74) that this 'clerk' or 'scribe' may be the evangelist himself; having taken up what was then the discreditable profession of a commercial clerk, he was later (after his conversion) able to turn his talents to good use in another form of writing. The grammar of the phrase is unclear, and one may wonder whether, despite the example of Kafka, the experience of a commercial clerk is likely to have prepared a man for a career as a writer. However that may be, if the aphorism implies, as it seems to, that a disciple is one who has received instruction in the kingdom of heaven, then this is certainly a rather tamer version of the kingdom of heaven than Jesus' orginal call to total conversion.

In any case, it is characteristic of Matthew's view of the Christian message that instruction in the kingdom should issue in action. What kind of action? Matthew sums it up in the word *'dikaiosyne'* (justice or righteousness). It is typical of him that after quoting Jesus' traditional injunction to 'seek the kingdom of God' he should straightaway add 'and his righteousness' (6.33). Righteousness can be said to be the fruit of instruction in the kingdom and in a looser sense to be identical with the kingdom itself. The insistence on the need to bear fruit is typical of this gospel (e.g. 7.16-20); and whereas John, in the allegory of the vine, insists that the first condition of fruitfulness is attachment to the person of Christ, Matthew is concerned above all with the need for catechesis. In the explanation of the parable of the sower, where Mark's version refers to hearing and *acceptance* of the word, Matthew reads: 'he who hears the word and *understands* it' (Mt 13.23; Mk 4.20). And understanding presupposes instruction. (The two ideas are directly connected in 13.51f.) It is those who keep on listening to the word in order to grasp it more fully who bear fruit, 'in one case a hundredfold, in another sixty, in another thirty' (13.23). This must also be borne in mind when we are interpreting Matthew's highly personal conclusion to the parable of the wicked husbandmen: 'Therefore, I tell you, the kingdom of God will be taken from you and given to a nation producing the fruits of it' (Mt 21.43).

To trace the development of the idea of the kingdom of God from its origins in the preaching of Jesus to its absorption by the teaching Church would be an interesting, though difficult, task. Matthew, of course, preserves the living tradition of Jesus' preaching of the kingdom as an imminent, ineluctable force, one that is already mysteriously present (cf. Mt 11.12; 12.28) as a personal challenge. But since the time of Jesus, something of the mystery and dynamism of this concept has evaporated. For Matthew himself it has lost most of the harsh, eschatological flavour it originally possessed. The kingdom of heaven is now the treasure of the Church's teaching about Jesus, the central object of the faith, the driving-force behind her moral teaching; it *belongs* to the Church, not of course after the fashion of a precious stone, pretty but inert, but as the vital instrument through which the Church's missionaries would set out to convert the world, though now it implies instruction as well as proclamation. Like the Jewish concept of the Torah (law), which it resembles and up to a point replaces, the kingdom is both a gift and a burden, even though compared with the regulations imposed by the Pharisees the burden is light (Mt 11.30) and shouldering it brings rest to the soul. It is a sign of God's favour, but one which carries with it the obligation of 'fulfilling all justice'. It is not, therefore, a gift in the Pauline sense: for Paul, righteousness is a grace, and it is the gift itself which carries justification and the possibility of acting righteously before God. For Matthew, 'imperative and indicative are one' (G. Strecker, *Der Weg der Gerechtigkeit,* 1966, p. 175), in the sense that the teaching itself is Jesus' summons to action.

So it is that the eschatological power of the proclamation of the kingdom is harnessed to the teaching of the law. This does not mean that the eschatological is entirely engulfed in the ethical; rather, the imperative to 'seek after justice' is stressed because it is the way to attain to the kingdom. Justice and righteousness are present possibilities; the kingdom belongs to the future. Like justice, it can be striven after, but unlike justice, it cannot, even in principle, be fully attained.

Jesus' final commission to his disciples after the Resurrection is also the evangelist's last word. In it he sums up the central teaching of his gospel: (1) that in the reign of Jesus his own teaching concerning the coming of the kingdom is being realized; (2) that the Church, in carrying out her task of preaching and baptizing, is the true heir to the promises of old; (3) that the essence of the Christian mission is to make disciples of all mankind – disciples, that is, in the sense that has emerged in the main body of the gospel, men taught 'to observe all I have commanded you,' men prepared to be 'just' for Christ's sake and to show by their harvest of good works that the seed of his word has fallen upon fertile soil.

Matthew's gospel ends without so much as a hint of Jesus' subsequent Ascension. What interests him is not the heavenly majesty of the Son of God, but the earthly power of the Risen Jesus (though the absoluteness of that power is, of course, determined by the fact that his authority extends over heaven as well as earth). The Lord's definitive departure from this world is a self-evident fact; what impresses Matthew, however, is the much more mysterious and intangible fact of his continuing presence. So he is anxious to bequeath to his readers his own faith in the unwearying activity of the Risen Lord on behalf of his Church, not just in view of an unseen future, the world to come, but here and now. The last word of the gospel, 'age', also means 'world'.

Matthew insists that the time of Jesus' full authority is now, and that the place where he exercises it is the world.

77

CHAPTER 6

THE FOURTH GOSPEL

The early Christians were keenly aware of the striking differences between the fourth gospel and the other three, and
the basis of their expositions of John's purpose was invariably, as Maurice Wiles has observed, Clement's dictum that
it is intended to be 'a *"pneumatikon euangelion"* (spiritual
gospel), in supplementation of the earlier ones whose con-
centration had been upon *"ta somatika"* (the bodily – or
perhaps we may translate – the naked facts)'. Naked facts,
only waiting to be clothed in spiritual meanings – a monu-
mental misinterpretation and a potentially disastrous one,
though the metaphor itself is modern. The truth is that the
fourth gospel is the most sophisticated and elaborate example of the genre known to us. In it, the possibilities of the
gospel form are exploited to the full, and its implications
exposed and commented upon.

We may start by recalling a point that was made in an
earlier chapter (p. 60). Why, if John was concerned less with
facts than with meanings, did he choose to write a gospel in
the first place? Why could he not have said all he wanted in
letters, as St Paul had done before him and as one of his
close collaborators (the author of the Johannine epistles)
was to do after him? Käsemann, as we have seen, answered
this question by pointing out the inadequacy of Bultmann's
view of John as a theologian uninterested in the historical
Jesus. For 'if one has absolutely no interest in the historical
Jesus, then one does not write a gospel' at all (*New Testament Questions of Today* (1969) p. 41).

The gap opened up by form criticism between the Jesus
of history and the Christ of faith was precisely the gap the
gospel writers were concerned to close. They had all seen,
or at any rate sensed, our modern problem and were trying,
each in his own way, to answer it. The danger of adhering
too closely to the form-critical method is that its aims may

come to be identified, in some totally muddled und unre-flective way, with those of the evangelists. Or rather, the method runs the risk of ignoring that the gospels were given the highly characteristic structure we associate with the word 'gospel' not in the haphazard way that a boy sticks stamps into an album, but for a definite reason. In fact, the evangelists were interested neither in what we call the Jesus of history nor in what Bultmann calls the Christ of faith, but in Jesus Christ, the single object of our faith. The fun-damental affirmations of the Christian belief were, as we have seen, 'Jesus is the Christ' and 'Jesus is Lord'. And the evangelists' concern was precisely to hold together Jesus of Nazareth and the risen Christ in this single affirmation, an act of judgment in the sense of Maréchal and Lonergan, but above all an act of faith. They were neither historians nor theologians, but combined the functions of both in declaring their own faith and eliciting the faith of their readers. It would not be too far from the truth to say that the main trouble with nineteenth-century biblical scholarship was that it searched the gospels for history, whereas the main trouble of post-Bultmannian exegesis is that it has searched the gos-pels for theology. Nothing could have been further from the intention of the evangelists than to fulfil what von Ranke conceived to be the historian's function *par excellence*, to record what actually happened; they are certainly more like theologians than historians; but to speak of them as primari-ly theologians is a dangerous half-truth.

Käsemann's position was anticipated and carefully de-fended by Sir Edwyn Hoskyns in the introduction to his commentary on the fourth gospel, which appeared posthu-mously in 1940. The purpose of his commentary is, he says, to barricade the roads which seek to solve the problem of the meaning of the gospel

either by regarding this Meaning as an idea of the author or as something which itself belongs to the mere hearing or sight of an eyewitness, regarded as a historian, for in that case his faith would be not mere-ly irrelevant, but actually suspect, since the eyewit-nesses who believed could not be accepted as an impartial witness. The purpose of this commentary is also to barricade the roads which lead to a distangling of history and interpretation. This triple barricading does not, however, originate in some perversity of the author of the commentary, but because these barricades have been erected by the original author of the book, and the meaning of his book must remain closed to those who tear down the barricades which he has so carefully erected. Did we say that he erected these barricades? No, we must not say this. He found the barricades there already, for he is persuaded that the meaning which he has heard does veritably lie in the history. Without it the history is meaningless. Take away the meaning and we should have merely the record of an eyewitness. Take away the history and we should be left only with a human notion or idea (*The Fourth Gospel*, p. 132).

How is it, then, that John achieves his purpose? He does so by operating constantly on two levels of understanding. There is one level at which the story of Jesus' life and death is accessible to any reader, ancient or modern, believer or unbeliever. This is quite precisely the level of the *story*, the *events*. There is a second level which is accessible only to the believer, looking back on these events in the light of the Resurrection. On the first level, the events recorded belong to the *past*: on the second level they belong to the *present:* or better, the past is *made present* by the Spirit. This is the key to John's gospel, a key whose use and usefulness he explains from time to time in the course of the book.

The idea of a two-tier revelation was a familiar theme of the contemporary Jewish apocalyptic. John's adaptation of this idea is strikingly original, but the idea itself was widespread and crops up in one form or another throughout the New Testament. In apocalyptic literature there is first of all a distinction between two *types* of revelation, one shadowy and original, given in a vision or a dream, the other clear and explicit, usually consisting of an interpretation of the mysterious vision or dream. The Book of Daniel is full of examples of visions or dreams whose significance is only dimly perceived by the person to whom they are vouchsafed and has to be expounded subsequently by a prophet or seer.

The second distinction that can be drawn concerns not two *types* but two *times* of revelation, and consequently two sets of people to whom the revelation is granted. Very often, this distinction between two times is sharpened to a point where it becomes necessary to speak of two *epochs* or *ages*. In the first epoch there is a revelation which is reserved to a few just men, prophets or visionaries especially favoured by God. During this time the world as a whole remains in the dark, and the mystery disclosed to a few continues to be hidden from the rest of mankind. In the apocalyptic tradition itself, this distinction between the few and the many is a feature of the present age. Only in the age to come, *ha'olam habba'*, will the mystery be made manifest to all. A good example of this belief is to be found at Qumrân, where the community, convinced that it had been privileged to receive the revelation of the New Covenant, apparently made no attempt to communicate the revelation to those outside.

The Christian adaptation of this distinction between the two ages is marked by a conviction that the world to come is with us now, that the kingdom of God has arrived and is among us. A particularly striking example occurs right at the end of St Paul's letter to the Romans: 'Now to him who is able to strengthen you according to my gospel and the preaching of Jesus Christ, according to the revelation of the mystery which was kept secret for long ages but is now disclosed and through the prophetic writings is made known to all nations, according to the command of the eternal God, to bring about obedience to the faith – to the only wise God be glory for evermore through Jesus Christ! Amen' (Rom 16.25-27). The Marcan Messianic secret, implying as it does that during Jesus' lifetime much must remain hidden and that the time of full revelation will come only after his death, harnesses this distinction to the gospel form. As we have seen, the reasons for Jesus' extreme and rather puzzling discretion within this gospel are to be sought not only

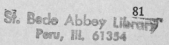

in the bitter opposition of the Pharisees, which certainly invited prudence, nor in Jesus' reluctance to see a false interpretation put upon his claim, but above all in the incapacity of Jesus' hearers to grasp the real meaning of the events they were witnessing without the aid of the Spirit. And until their minds and hearts were flooded with the light of the Resurrection (or alternatively and equivalently the light of the Spirit) they could not reach an understanding of who Jesus was.

It is left to John to work out the divine logic of this revelation of the Spirit: 'If anyone is thirsty, let him come to me; and let him who believes in me drink. As the Scripture says, out of his belly shall flow rivers of living water' (Jn 7.39). This solemn proclamation is interpreted as referring to 'the Spirit which those who were to believe in him were to receive; for there was as yet no Spirit, because Jesus was not yet glorified' (7.40). 'Glory' in the fourth gospel refers sometimes, as here, to the Passion and Resurrection taken together as a single mystery, sometimes to the Incarnation and the signs which accompanied it. But the Resurrection is the condition of the reception of the Spirit, because during Jesus' lifetime 'there was as yet no Spirit' (that is, according to the early theology of Acts 2.33, the Spirit had not yet been received by Jesus for pouring out on others). So on the first level of understanding the water is a metaphor for the *word,* the revelation of Jesus (as it is in the conversation with the Samaritan woman in ch. 4). Jesus invites his hearers to come and drink from the fountain of the living word. On the second level of understanding, the one to which the evangelist draws attention, the word and the Spirit are inseparable. In accepting the word of Jesus in faith, the believer receives the Spirit, and conversely it is the function of the Spirit to teach and remind the disciples of the message of Jesus.

There is, then, a real sense in which Jesus revealed the truth while on earth. But his revelation was limited by the circumstances of his human incarnation. The full revelation is the Incarnation manifested in the light of the Spirit. 'These things I have spoken to you while I am still with you. But the Paraclete, the Holy Spirit, whom the Father will send in my name, he will teach you [i.e. explain to you] all things, and bring to your remembrance all that I have said to you' (Jn 14.25f.). 'Bring to remembrance' – not to add anything new, but to recall. But remembrance is not simply a question of flashing a recorded image on to an inner screen. Suddenly, one remembers, and in remembering grasps the full significance of the event or remark for the first time: 'Ah, now I understand what he meant when he said...'

The best known example of what this reminding involves is the story of the journey to Emmaus, where Jesus explained to the two wayfarers the significance of the Scriptures which foretold his own passion and death. But their eyes were held and they failed to recognize him. When they eventually *did* recognize him, in the breaking of the bread, they realized for the first time what he meant when he was discoursing to them on the road about the Scriptures, and they said, 'Did not our hearts burn within us?' (Lk 24.32). The answer is, of course, they did and they didn't. No doubt they had some obscure sense of the importance of the occasion, but it was only when their eyes were opened and they *saw* – in the light of the Resurrection – what he meant, that they were able to interpret this feeling as 'their hearts burning within them'. So Luke conveys symbolically the enlightenment brought by the Resurrection. Only by recognizing Jesus, and seeing him in their past, could they be led to a full understanding of the Scriptures concerning him.

The clearest example of the same phenomenon in the fourth gospel follows the story of the cleansing of the temple, which is recounted much earlier on in Jesus' career than it can actually have occurred so as to allow both Passion and Resurrection to be foreshadowed together towards the beginning of the work. 'Destroy this temple,' says Jesus, 'and in three days I will raise it up'. The evangelist interprets this saying of 'the temple of his body', and adds, 'When therefore he was raised from the dead, his disciples remembered that he had said this; and they believed the scripture and the word which Jesus had spoken' (Jn 2. 19-

22). Most Catholic commentators accept this interpretation as it stands. But how were Jesus' audience supposed to divine his meaning? There is nothing either in his words or in the situation in which they were spoken which would assist his hearers to make the imaginative leap from temple to body. If he was really referring to his own body, then he was doing so in such an obscure and roundabout way that all blame for the ensuing misunderstanding must lie with him. Unless perhaps, as one desperate exegete has suggested, he pointed to himself as he spoke! All becomes clear once we allow for two levels of understanding, first the level of Jesus' first hearers, secondly the level of the readers of the gospel. The disciples understand only when they remember, and we must conclude that they are reminded by the Spirit, who at the same time shows the relevance of Jesus' words to their new situation.

The explanation of the systematic ambiguities with which the gospel is studded must lie in the same direction: 'When I am lifted up from the earth I will draw all men to myself' (12.32). The lifting up had a double reference, first to the Resurrection and Ascension, which the crowd fail to understand because of prejudices about the Messiah ('We have heard from the law that the Christ remains for ever'), and secondly to the Crucifixion. But the understanding of the Cross is given only with the Resurrection, without which no one can feel the drawing power of Calvary. Similarly, when Caiaphas prophesied that Jesus should die for the nation the full significance of his prophecy was not available to the Sanhedrin whom he was addressing.

Sometimes the device is less obvious. Who, for instance, are the Greeks who went up to Jerusalem to celebrate the Passover (Jn 12.20)? Some commentators maintain that they are Jewish proselytes, coming from the cities of the Hellenistic diaspora; others say that the evangelist is stressing the universal significance of what is about to take place during this feast. Both are right; but on different levels of understanding. A very striking example of the same technique is furnished by the judgment scene before Pilate. On one level Jesus is a condemned criminal, on the second the judge of all mankind. And when Pilate brings Jesus out to pass sentence (19.13) the Greek is ambiguous. On the first level of understanding the verb is intransitive and implies that Pilate himself sat on the judgment seat, on the second level it is transitive, and implies that he sat Jesus down, making *him* the one to pronounce the verdict on his own accusers. Impossible to convey in translation, this ambiguity deliberately evokes one of the main arguments of this gospel, that by rejecting the word of Jesus men bring condemnation on themselves and encompass their own destruction.

So it is with the whole gospel: 'I have said this to you in riddles; the hour is coming when I shall no longer speak to you in riddles but tell you plainly of the Father' (Jn 16.25). Jesus is still the Revealer, but this second and more important revelation will be carried through by the mediation of the Spirit. When Jesus departs from the world he will continue to teach and preach, but he will no longer be physically present. He will be spiritually present, personally present, since where the Spirit of the Lord is, there the Lord is also. 'I have yet many things to say to you, but you cannot bear them now. When the Spirit of truth comes, he will guide you all into the truth; for he will not speak on his own authority, but whatever he hears he will speak, and he will declare to you the things that are to come' (Jn 16.12f.). Just as it is the Father who works in Jesus (5.19-30), in such a way that 'he who has seen me has seen the Father' (14.9), so the teaching of Jesus will receive its full expression in that of the Holy Spirit. What was veiled will then be made plain, not just to the apostles who have actually seen the living Jesus but also to generations yet unborn who will know him only through faith. And it is these, those who have not seen but yet have believed (20.29), who are the true contemporaries of Jesus.

But however important the experience of the Resurrection must be counted for the understanding of the significance of Jesus' teaching and of the way he lived and died, revelation did not stop there. We have seen that throughout the period intervening between the death of Jesus and the composition of the first gospel there was a constant process of adjustment and application. The form critics focused a spotlight on this hitherto very obscure period, obscure because the very nature of the sources tends to cover up the gap between the physical existence of Jesus of Nazareth and his spiritual presence within the Christian community. So the gospel form, as I have argued, was designed to close this gap, and to affirm in a very practical way the traditional faith that the Jesus spoken of by Christian teachers and preachers was both Christ and Lord or, conversely, that the Lord whom they worshipped in their prayers and liturgical services was Jesus of Nazareth. So his words and actions, recorded in the tradition, were seen to cast light on the new situation in which the community found itself: sometimes the problem was the growth of a dissentient group, at others oppression and persecution from outside, at others (as we see very clearly in Mt 23) the arrogance and vanity of those members of the community who have been entrusted with a certain authority – the clergy. The contribution of the fourth gospel was not to devise a method of exhibiting Jesus' continued presence but to systematize one that already existed. The author has evidently reflected on the theoretical implications of the form he has adopted and his reflections take the form of a theology of the Spirit.

From a formal point of view, then, the author of the fourth gospel stands at the end of a literary tradition, in much the same way as Joyce and Proust stand at the end of the tradition of the nineteenth-century novel. He, like them, has not only included in his work comments on the form he has inherited, but taken the special techniques inherent in the form further than ever before. But what is true of form is equally true of content. In John's theology of revelation hints and guesses scattered throughout the other three gospels come to fruition. The synoptic gospels make it plain that the main burden of Jesus' own preaching was the kingdom of God. Tentatively identified by Mark with the person of Jesus and by Matthew with his ethical teaching, this notion gives way in the fourth gospel to the mystery of revelation itself. And the revelation is simply Christ and his own essential being, which is to be the Son of the Father, sent into the world by him to bear witness to the truth. Conversely, this truth is none other than Christ himself. The real irony of Pilate's famous question is that truth in person stood before him as he wondered. Jesus is himself the revealer *par excellence* and the object of his own revelation: 'mediator simul et plenitudo totius revelationis' (*Dei Verbum*, 2).

According to Bultmann, the revelation of Christ in the fourth gospel is restricted to the fact that he is the Revealer: 'John presents only the fact (*das Dass*) of Revelation, without illustrating its content (*ihr Was*)' (*Theologie des NT*, p. 419). With a truly Kantian repugnance for the messy, uncontrollable data of the phenomenal (i.e. historical) world and a longing for a direct communication with the Revealer that does not need to be channelled through a heteronomous magisterium, Bultmann envisages faith as the term of an encounter with an exiguous Christ, pared down to the ultimate essence of a word. So in some respects Bultmann's conception of the word of God is the antithesis of John's. Where Bultmann narrows, John enlarges, so as to embrace the whole of the life and teaching of Jesus, which in its turn has gathered up the whole of the Old Testament revelation.

The images and symbols employed by John exhibit both manner and meaning of Jesus' message. He is the light shining in the darkness, the living water, the path to the Father, the shepherd and the vine. Man's necessities as well as God's goodness become plain, since all the symbols are comprehensible only in a human context. The cripple, the blind man groping in the dark, the lifeless corpse, images of the human condition without God, are the almost necessary correlatives of the way, the light and the life. They enrich the message without distracting from it. It is the truth (or the word) that looses the bonds of sin, so that one can walk again: 'the truth will set you free' (8.32); 'You are already made clean by the word which I have spoken to you' (15.3). It is the truth that unseals the eyes, so that one can distinguish between the right and the wrong, the ugly and the beautiful, and go through life without stumbling incessantly: 'For judgment I came into this world, that those who

87

do not see may see...' (9.39). It is the truth, finally, that gives life, a special sort of life no doubt, but one in which all the qualities of life – energy, movement, vigorous activity and social communication – play their part: 'Truly, truly, I say to you, he who hears my word and believes him who sent me, has eternal life' (5.24).

Christ is thus indistinguishable from his word ('I *am* the truth'); and so when we say, with John, that the truth does all these things we are responding to a person. We are accepting the special relationship that obtains between Jesus and his followers, the Revealer and the faithful believers. And the remarkable fact is that this relationship sheds light both on what we are and on what God is, our poverty and his abundance. We cannot separate out God from his revelation by a process analogous to chemical precipitation any more than we can separate the dancer from the dance. Our God is a God who reveals himself and we cannot know him as any other. If Christ is both the image of the Father and the fulness of revelation, its totally adequate object, then for us God is a self-manifesting God. To accept his revelation in faith is to accept, as Bultmann insists, the creator-creature relationship, which is, by its structure, a preliminary and unformulated demand for faith. That is to say, creation and revelation are the same sort of act: creation is a sort of revelation, revelation is a sort of creation; only the level is different. Both are carried out through the mediation of the Word, the Image of God. So in according Christ our faith we permit him to re-establish a relationship that had been broken by man's claim to independence. And we know God, in Christ, as Creator and Revealer.

But, *pace* Bultmann, this knowledge is knowledge in the proper sense of the word. Enjoying the dance, we applaud the dancer, hearing the song, we clap the singer. Existential and ontological are interwoven. No doubt we first meet Christ in his role as mediator of revelation-salvation *for us* (how could it be otherwise?); but far from exhausting the *being* of Christ, this role simply exhibits it in a way we can understand. He is the Word made Flesh, the Son of God made man, and the life of the spirit to which he introduces us is the life of his own Spirit, the third person of the Trinity. The mutual relationship of the three persons is displayed in the Incarnation of the Son, as the early Fathers, who regularly argued from the economy of salvation towards the ontological reality lying behind it, saw so well. And the Holy Spirit is bestowed on us by Christ precisely because and in so far as we are introduced to the Father and so share in the living intercommunication between Father and Son which *is* the Spirit.

But if the life of the Spirit is to endure there must be an unbroken contact with Jesus. To show this, John has written a book which can be read in two ways, either as a story of Jesus' life (and even on this level the events constitute a coherent narrative) or as a challenge to belief (and on this level the narrative has a *spiritual* cohesion). But the spiritual significance is not detachable from the narrative: what is being interpreted for us is the earthly life of Christ. And in living out his earthly destiny he is by that very act deciding the ultimate fate of mankind, triumphing over the forces of darkness. The two roles of the Son of Man, to suffer on earth and to conquer in heaven, are united.

SHORT BIBLIOGRAPHY

GENERAL

Barclay, W., *The First Three Gospels*, London, S.P.C.K. (1966)

Bea, A., *The Study of the Synoptic Gospels. New Approaches and Outlooks,* London, Chapman (1965)

Neil, S., *The Interpretation of the New Testament 1861-1961,* London, O.U.P. (1964)

Léon-Dufour, X., *The Gospels and the Jesus of History,* London, Collins (1968)

CHAPTER 1

Schweitzer, A., *The Quest of the Historical Jesus,* London, A. and C. Black (3rd edition, 1954)

Kähler, M., *The so called Historical Jesus and the Historic, Biblical Christ,* Philadelphia, Fortress Press (1964)

Robinson, J.M., *A New Quest of the Historical Jesus,* London, S.C.M. Press (1959)

Anderson, H., *Jesus and Christian Origins,* New York, O.U.P. (1964)

CHAPTER 2

Bultmann, R., *The History of the Synoptic Tradition,* London, Basil Blackwell (2nd edition, 1968)

Dibelius, M., *From Tradition to Gospel,* London, Ivor Nicholson and Watson (1934)

Lightfoot, R.H., *History and Interpretation in the Gospels,* London, Hodder and Stoughton (1935)

Taylor, V., *The Formation of the Gospel Tradition,* London, Macmillan (1933)

Rohde, E., *Rediscovering the Teaching of the Evangelists,* London, S.C.M. Press (1968) (on redaction criticism)

CHAPTER 3

Taylor, V., *The Life and Ministry of Jesus,* London, Macmillan (1954)

Bornkamm, G., *Jesus of Nazareth,* London, Hodder and Stoughton (1960)

Barrett, C.K., *Jesus and the Gospel Tradition,* London, S.P.C.K. (1967)

Flusser, D., *Jesus,* New York, Herder and Herder (1968)

Jeremias, J., *New Testament Theology, Volume One, The Proclamation of Jesus,* London, S.C.M. Press (1971)

CHAPTER 4

Evans, C.F., *The Beginning of the Gospel...* London, S.P.C.K. (1968) (on Mark)

Nineham, D., *Saint Mark,* London, Penguin (1963)

Martin, R.P., *Mark, Evangelist and Theologian,* Exeter, Paternoster (1973)

Fenton, J.C., *Saint Matthew,* London, Penguin (1963)

Marshall, I.H., *Luke, Historian and Theologian,* Exeter, Paternoster (1970)

CHAPTER 5

Of the large number of available commentaries, the most outstanding are those by Rudolf Bultmann and Raymond Brown. But there is much to be learnt from books by Sir Edwyn Hoskyns and C.H. Dodd. The references are:

Hoskyns, E., *The Fourth Gospel,* London, Faber and Faber (1947)

Bultmann, R., *The Gospel of John,* Oxford, Basil Blackwell (1971)

Dodd, C.H., *The Interpretation of the Fourth Gospel,* Cambridge University Press (1953)

Dodd, C.H., *Historical Tradition and the Fourth Gospel,* Cambridge University Press (1965)

Brown, R.E., *The Gospel according to John,* New York, Doubleday, Vols. I (1966) and II (1970)

INDEX

THEOLOGY TODAY SERIES

27 THE THEOLOGY OF THE EUCHARIST
BY JAMES QUINN, S.J.

The Eucharist is the Heart of the Christian life. It is the sacrament of Christ's presence because it is the sacrament of his sacrifice. It is the summary, the sign and the means of salvation.
In celebrating the Eucharist we stand before the Father in joyful praise of all his wonderful works. The presence of Christ, and our unity in him, enables us to offer to the Father perfect praise and thanksgiving. Christ is himself the mighty act of God in history, the One whose body is the centre of the new liturgy in spirit and truth.

At the Eucharist Christ sends the Holy Spirit to build up the Church as his body and to make the world a temple to God's glory. The reconciling work of the Eucharist brings unity to creation.
    The Eucharist prepares the Church on earth for the glory of heaven. It is the joyful sign of the second Coming of Christ. It is the beginning, the firstfruits, of the transfiguration of the material universe into a new world wholly dominated by the risen Christ.

43 THE CHURCH AND THE WORLD
BY RODGER CHARLES, S.J.

The claim of the secularising theologians or those who popularise what they say, is summed up by the statement of Bonhoeffer concerning the rejection of the religious premise and man's coming of age. In popular discussion, it seems to the author, this is taken to mean that by rejecting many of the external forms and the positive beliefs of Christianity man mysteriously becomes more Christian. But Christianity only had its impact on history because of those externals and beliefs, which were not contradictory to the spirit of Christ in the Church but a manifestation of it. Further, the very things which Western man is most proud of are a result of his

Christian inheritance, an inheritance which he owes to the labours of traditional Christianity, strengthened and guided by its dogma, through hundreds of years. It is not secularisation which will save modern man from his present predicament. It is a return to and a strengthening of the values and the institutions of traditional Christianity.

33 THE PRIEST AS PREACHER, PAST AND FUTURE BY EDWARD P. ECHLIN, S.J.

What is a priest? This is a question often asked today when the existence of an educated and devout laity, the variety of tasks open to the priest and the existence of a married diaconate have all combined to blur the traditional lines between priest and people. Is a priest's primary duty to offer the sacrifice of the Mass and to forgive sins? Is it more secular pastoral work? Should a priest be engaged in a secular profession?

Fr. Echlin's answer is that a priest is first and foremost a preacher of the word of God. All his other duties follow from this. The author establishes this point by a thorough examination of the historical development of the priesthood, giving careful attention to the liturgies and theological writings of the early and medieval Church.

The investigation throws a light on the evolution of the power of the priesthood and the episcopate. This point can revolutionise the search for reunion with the Churches, the validity of whose orders the Catholic Church has traditionally been unable to accept.

First published in the Netherlands
Made and printed by Van Boekhoven-Bosch N.V., Utrecht